Nurturing Brilliance

# NURTURING BRILLIANCE

## Using Play-Activated Learning to Awaken Children's Potential

Sally Fowler Haughey

Redleaf Press®
www.redleafpress.org
800-423-8309

Published by Redleaf Press
10 Yorkton Court
St. Paul, MN 55117
www.redleafpress.org



First edition 2025
Cover design by Louise OFarrell
Cover photograph by Holly Button
Interior design by Douglas Schmitz
Typeset in Chapparal Pro
Interior photos by Holly Button
Printed in the United States of America
32 31 30 29 28 27 26 25 1 2 3 4 5 6 7 8

Library of Congress Cataloging-in-Publication Data
Names: Haughey, Sally author
Title: Nurturing brilliance : using play-activated learning to awaken children's potential / by Sally Fowler Haughey.
Description: First edition. | St. Paul, MN : Redleaf Press, 2025. | Includes bibliographical references and index. | Summary: "Acclaimed educator Sally Haughey has distilled decades of research and experience to create the Play-Activated Learning model for understanding children's play and learning and nurturing their innate brilliance. Explaining the incredible unfolding and blossoming that happens during play, Nurturing Brilliance provides a science-based approach to communicating that growth and development to parents, while highlighting the expert you already are and providing you a way to bridge gaps in understanding so that all well-intended parties can support the ultimate goal-children's growth and learning"— Provided by publisher.
Identifiers: LCCN 2025003683 (print) | LCCN 2025003684 (ebook) | ISBN 9781605548357 paperback | ISBN 9781605548364 ebook
Subjects: LCSH: Play--Psychological aspects | Child development | Activity programs in education | Early childhood education
Classification: LCC LB1139.35.P55 H42 2025 (print) | LCC LB1139.35.P55 (ebook) | DDC 649/.5--dc23/eng/20250327
LC record available at https://lccn.loc.gov/2025003683
LC ebook record available at https://lccn.loc.gov/2025003684

Printed on acid-free paper

*To those who have passed but are not gone from my daily thoughts:*
*My sister Chris, my best friend Amy, and my parents,*
*MaryJane and Arlen. You are missed beyond measure.*

# CONTENTS

# Acknowledgments

First and foremost, thank you to my partner, John, for all of the support and meals while I wrote this book. Without him, it would not have been possible. This book took a year longer than I anticipated, and John never wavered in his belief in this project. Thank you, my love, for your constant love and guidance.

Thank you to Melissa York, my editor at Redleaf, for her mad skills. Because of her, this book is more consistent and tightly focused. Her job title should read Book Fairy because she added such magical tweaks and edits. I am in awe of her talent.

A huge thank you to Laura Nicholls, my book midwife, for making me sound better and helping me when I was in a rut unable to move forward. Giving birth to a book is harder than I expected, and she helped me when it mattered the most. Laura took my words, sprinkled magic, and made them sing. I will forever be grateful.

A million thanks to my team, Abbey, Jill, Jelalia, Leslie, and Sara, who believed in my book and gave me the space to write it (that is, endured delayed responses)!

A heartfelt thank you to all of the children in my career by whom I was so privileged to be called "teacher." In truth, they were my teachers, and I am forever grateful for the wisdom of play they taught me.

Finally, I would like to offer a toast of gratitude to all the educators, family care providers, homeschool parents, principals, and child care owners worldwide who have supported my work. I would not be who I am today without you. I am indebted to you all.

CHAPTER 1

# What Is Play-Activated Learning?

A child without education is like a bird without wings.
—Anonymous

In the summer of 1996, I was obsessed with designing my very first classroom. When I walked into the space, it looked as if it was frozen in time. The furniture and area rugs were from the 1960s. The room felt battered and worn. Dated laminated posters of the alphabet and numbers hung on the wall. It was all so ugly and disheartening; it would surely kill any child's desire to learn.

Filled with anticipation, I excitedly doodled ideas on paper. I configured nearly twenty ways to set up the room until my mind was reeling with all of the wonderful possibilities. I immediately set about finding every garage sale within a five-mile radius, looking for unusual objects and furniture. Slowly, the room began to take shape. By the time school started, I felt so ready and inspired—I'd literally spent three months preparing.

The first day of school, I waited eagerly as eighteen preschool children arrived. I will never forget calling the children to the carpet for Morning Meeting that first time. As my voice rang out, eighteen pairs of eyes met mine. *Instantly and without question.* I realized in that moment that it was such a privilege to have their trust. And clearly, I was someone important.

The second week of school, one of the mothers asked me, "When are you going to start the worksheets? When is my son going to learn how to write letters?"

Another parent inquired, "What reading program are you going to use?"

My jaw must have hit my chest. These were four-year-olds in a Mother's Day Out program at a church. Formal reading? Formal letter writing? Really? I never in my wildest dreams imagined these would be the concerns of the parents. Clearly, these parents didn't recognize play as a valid pathway of learning. They didn't get it.

I started to question myself. Am I wrong? Am I missing something? Am I doing the right thing? Parents' expectations ate away at my confidence. These parents were *not looking* for rich play-based environments to nurture their child's natural brilliance but rather were *expecting* academic-based environments. Academics were held in high esteem, and I had no idea how to help them see the immense value and developmental appropriateness of the work I was doing with children.

Four years later, I started working in a purportedly play-based program that served children who were considered "at risk." The first week there, my supervisor ordered me to put up a word wall for three-year-olds and label everything in my classroom with printed words. All light switches needed to be labeled "Light Switch," the doors "Door," and so on for all the other hundred items in my room. I was dumbfounded. Filling my room with hundreds of labels flew in the face of all the research I had been doing that showed how important it is that posted words create a meaningful connection for children. I had also just come out of a three-year training in Waldorf education in which we discussed the negative effect of visual noise in the classroom. I knew the children didn't need all that visual clutter, especially given that many of them were unable to recognize letters. Environmental print should be meaningful to the children.

My supervisor's request for a word wall for three-year-olds was my final tipping point—I knew I needed to find a way to explain the irreplaceable benefits of play-based learning. I decided to arm myself with as much knowledge about play as I could. I read hundreds of books and articles and took every course I could find. When I shared this massive paradigm shift with families, however, their eyes would glaze over. It wasn't making the difference or having the impact I'd hoped it would. I realized the problem wasn't about giving families piles of information. What I needed was a way to *show* families and administrators how play was not only the gold standard but also how children uncovered their unique strengths through play. So I set my intention to find a way to do just that.

One night I couldn't sleep. Earlier that day, I'd had a conversation with the mother of one of my students, and my mind was still spinning on it. I had tried to explain to her why it was good news that her son returned to play with blocks every day. Lying awake, I kept toying with the idea of what would happen if I broke down the phases of a child's engagement based on the brain science and research

I'd been reading. I wondered what it would look like to include my engagement with the child as an educator and all the potentially incredible implications of that for nurturing children's growth and learning. In the middle of the night, the Play-Activated Learning model was born.

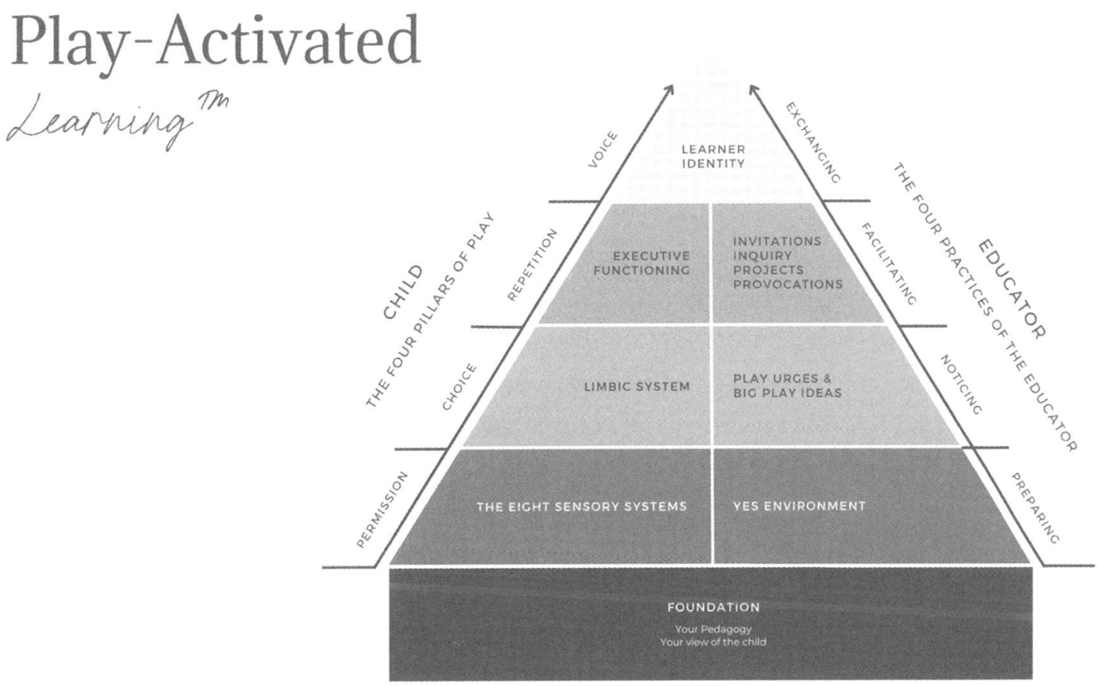


## THE PLAY-ACTIVATED LEARNING MODEL

The Play-Activated Learning model, or PAL model, helps you and families understand a child's behavior in the classroom during free play, including what is happening in the child's brain. The model offers a framework to explain the incredible growth and blossoming that happens during play. It provides a science-based approach to communicating that growth and development to families. It also provides insight on the educator's role in supporting a child's learning and development.

The hidden foundation of the PAL model is YOU: your beliefs, your role, and your views of the child, families, and education itself. In chapter 2 and later in chapter 6 we will take a deeper look at what your play-activated views are.

In this model are four essential markers or pillars of play engagement. Once you understand these phases, you have a powerful framework for articulating the learning happening in your setting. These pillars give us a view into the development of the child so we can best understand how to nurture the unfolding of their innate brilliance. To support this process, these pillars are accompanied by four core practices of the educator.

In the pages of this book, we'll explore in-depth the power and potential of play in supporting children's learning and cultivating their unique intelligence. Play alone, though, isn't the totality of the PAL model. It is the *practices* of the educator that lift it. It's the educator who's listening, observing, and asking for those exchanges with children that provide a vital view into their experience. It's the educator who chooses to understand children at a deeper level and who brings that understanding into application, putting a stake in the ground for what is supported by science and ultimately advocating for what is the healthiest and most appropriate and powerful way to educate children.

And, because you're here, dear reader, that educator is *you.* Let's take a look at what we will cover in each of the four pillars.

## Pillar 1: Permission

In chapter 3, we'll look at the teaching setting, whether it's the classroom, home, care center, or anywhere that children are learning and developing. Behind the scenes, we can create a yes environment that offers children permission to play with a wide variety of rich, sensory options. We'll also unpack how the amazing world of the environment relates to the eight sensory systems.

We'll take a look at why some children have difficulty choosing where to play ("I'm bored, there's nothing to do!"). You might see children crying, whining, wandering, refusing to play, or showing difficulty in transitioning between activities. Internally, however, the child is processing the environment and looking for what they might engage with. The educator's task is to create an environment of permission that supports the child's sensory needs.

## Pillar 2: Choice

When I was looking at the learning environments of my colleagues in traditional early childhood settings, I saw that *there was no real choice*. These centers were filled with teacher-directed activities and managed with population control or by rotating children through stations.

When a child first thinks, "Ah, I want to go to blocks—no, I want to go to dramatic play," and then decides, "I'm going to blocks," they're pushing away the distractions of the other choices. This builds executive control. It's how we learn to focus, plan, and attend to tasks. Most early childhood settings don't give children meaningful choice. In chapter 4, we will dive deep into why choice matters and how the educator can support this through the practice of noticing, including how we can set the stage for unbiased observation of children's big ideas and play urges.

## Pillar 3: Repetition

Have you ever had a child who wants to play the same thing day in and day out? Many educators mistakenly believe that children returning to the same activity over and over is a bad thing. In chapter 5, I'll share why it's a *brilliant* thing.

At this phase, the child is actively planning their play. They're walking into the environment and saying internally, "Okay, I'm going to blocks." And the next day, they say again, "Okay, I'm going to blocks." They're planning their play, choosing the same thing day in and day out—*intentionally.* The child is expressing a clear and definite preference.

It's human nature to repeat what we find pleasure in. The repetition of any activity strengthens the connections between neural pathways. It is increasing sustained focus and attention and thus building the foundation of executive functioning. So, my big tip to you here before we dive into this in more detail later is: trust repetitive play.

If you think about how a child rolls over, sits up, and eventually crawls, it's all leading to walking. In a similar way, repetitive play is preparing the child for higher-level thinking and play. We want to trust as a child chooses to return to the same activity again and again. Just as crawling leads to walking, repetitive play leads to a child's increasing capacity to construct deeper play. The educator supports this phase by spurring on children's interests and joy through things like invitations, provocations, and projects.

## Pillar 4: Voice

At this point in our model, the play's magic brings forth the fruits of academic preparation. Language is directly related to cognitive development, and at this stage of play, children are developing full expressive language. In chapter 6, I share the incredible potential of language. The educator supports this phase by exchanging ideas and perspectives with the child through conversations and Learning Stories, a narrative documentation method that develops their thinking processes.

Now a child is creating new ideas and transforming their play through new connections. They're actively forming ideas and theories for play. This innovative and creative stage requires time dedicated to free play. When I was teaching kindergarten in public school, many times I only had an hour or two for play. What made the difference and helped us use this limited time as valuably as possible was giving children free choice. By facilitating children's ability to choose, the stage is set for the development of their voice. They are empowered to explore what appeals to them most and thus communicate their interests and drives.

Brain science shows that when children have free choice, neural connections light up in a number of areas in the brain, including areas for motivation, innovation, and reflection (Diamond 2013). When children make choices, they are constructing their own meaning and their own understanding. It is in this process that children shine with their own unique brilliance. In mastering one area through repetition, children can then move on to the next, making complex connections that enable them to create and invent their own distinctive theories and ideas. Every year, I get teary-eyed when I see this happen in the room, because it's *contagious* as children influence one another in their play. This process, and the rich information it provides to us as educators, is truly a gift.

## THE PAL MODEL IN PRACTICE

I can't tell you, "Do this and it's going to work 100 percent of the time," but we can look to the PAL model for guidance and a framework. This model tells you what's happening in the brain, what's happening at the level of engagement, and what's happening at the level of facilitation and support. The secret to my system is what you do in response to each phase of child engagement.

There's no timetable for the phases of the PAL model. This is not a linear process. It's a spiral. The child can be at one phase and then move backward to another. This is not about where they "should" be. We can see the pathway they're on, and we honor and respect where they are. Just as when a child is starting to walk but then goes back to crawling, we don't say, "Don't crawl. Don't do that." Instead, we trust the process. It's a back-and-forth. Children process these developmental leaps in different and very individual ways. We want to honor this.

Each pillar of the PAL model supports the growth and development of a child's innate intelligence. We'll take a closer look at these "intelligences" in the final chapter of this book. You will find an even more profound understanding of how children's innate brilliance unfolds through play. To give context and meaning to the journey you're about to embark on, it's first important to understand what I mean by *innate brilliance*.

## The Innate Brilliance of Children

Many people associate the words *intelligence* and *brilliance* with some kind of academic measure, a sign of a high IQ or evolved cognitive ability. When we consider the innate brilliance of a child, however, we're not doing so in the context of these kinds of standards.

To best illustrate the nature of a child's inborn intelligence, I'm reminded of a boy in France named Christopher, whom I met in the early development of my online programs. His mother had chosen to homeschool him because he was clearly neurodivergent and she did not want him labeled and identified as autistic. She was seeking my support in educating her child within the rigid educational framework that was being imposed and trying to do her best to work with her child's needs while still "measuring up" to standards.

I coached Christopher's mother to follow his interests, to let *him* choose what he learned. He didn't learn to read until he was twelve, but by facilitating his play, interests, and joy, by age fourteen he had written three books about how to care for chickens, his deepest passion. Through this process, Christopher blossomed into his true self. His innate brilliance was nurtured and brought to light as he played and followed his chosen interests.

What is so magical and fascinating about play is that it does just this—it harnesses the innate intelligence of an individual not as it is measured against expectations or standards, but in that person's own fulfillment of life itself. We must ask ourselves: Why do we educate? I believe we should be educating children to give them the capacity to know who they are and what they want.

I recently had the pleasure and privilege of finding out that a former student of mine went on to become a botanist. When I think back on my time with her in her early childhood education, she was obsessed with plants. She noticed every single plant on the playground, and we created a recycled food garden with carrot tops and potato cuttings to cultivate her deepest passion. I'm not surprised, but I am delighted, to hear how her innate brilliance has blossomed in her adulthood.

We grow and iterate from the seeds of interest that are inside us as children, and it's a journey of discovery to what and who we become as adults. The greater point here is that we are born with our own composition and dispositions that move us toward our interests and what gives us joy.

The seeds of this innate intelligence may not always be clearly defined in children as a noun or topic. Consider a child who loves to be in the air—monkey bars, slides, or swinging from tree branches, for example. There's something moving there, a dynamic unfolding of the child's development, that we may not be able to detect but that is part of who they are and who they're becoming. Understanding this unfolding paves our way as educators to encourage children into their life ahead.

## Building Trust and Increasing Understanding

In my own practice, one of the amazing benefits I experienced was that the PAL model instantly builds trust with families, colleagues, and administrators. A story that comes immediately to mind took place during my second year as a kindergarten teacher. Every day after school, I would walk the children to the pickup line to go home. A bit of a trek led us through the cafeteria.

One day a few weeks into the school year, Eloise's father stormed through the building into the cafeteria and came right up to me. He was a body builder with threatening arms.

"Eloise hates school and has yet to come home with any homework or worksheets! I don't see any preparation for the first grade—or *anything* being done!" I could feel the heat of his breath and the eyes of all the other teachers and students looking at me as he shouted at me.

I grounded myself before answering. I thought: Why would he do this? It came in a flash.

"Eloise is so lucky to have a dad who cares as deeply as you."

I watched her dad relax, relieved that I had responded with intention and not reaction. This was not personal.

I put my hand on his arm and said, "Let me walk these children to the pickup, and afterward let's meet in my room to talk."

Back in the classroom, I sat down with Eloise's father and explained the brain science behind my approach. I pulled out worksheets from the school's purchased curriculum on trees and leaves and compared them to the inquiry we were engaged in using natural bark, branches, and leaves.

"Young children gather information from their senses. If we used worksheets to teach her about the change of the seasons, could she feel the difference between the red and orange leaves still on the tree versus those that have dropped and were turning brown? Think about materials holding the truth that our sensory system detects." I put the worksheet and a tray of leaves with magnifying glasses, scissors, and tweezers in front of him.

"I invite you to do the worksheet and then the activity and see how each experience informs your sense and understanding."

Eloise's father touched the worksheet and then the leaves, and nodded and said, "There is no comparison."

"Another important point is giving children a voice and vote over what we do. The children gathered the leaves we used from a walk in the schoolyard. They decided what tools we needed and helped construct our explorations. Involving their ideas in the process gives the children ownership and investment in the activity. This activates the limbic system, which is the light switch of learning. It is an emotional engagement."

I explained the role of choice in our classroom and why worksheets would only come home sometimes. Eloise's dad left my room thanking me for my approach. By the end of the year, he told me I was the best educator he had ever encountered. I'm not sure that is the truth, but what I can say is that I was probably one of the few teachers who ever took the time to explain to him why play is important and to show him how learning was unfolding in my classroom.

I realized then that parents, colleagues, and even administrators needed to be educated. They were caught in the assembly line approach that I'll be discussing in more depth in chapter 2. It was up to me to open their eyes.

Play isn't just a "good idea" for children. It's vital to their development, learning, and growth into healthy, functioning adults—so much so that psychiatrist and clinical researcher Stuart Brown warns that depriving children of play can have disastrous consequences. According to Dr. Brown, prolonged and significant lack of play, especially during the first decade of life, is associated with severe emotional dysregulation. This includes higher rates of depression, inflexible thinking patterns, reduced impulse control, diminished self-regulation, poor anger management, and weak, superficial long-term relationships. In his research, Brown interviewed twenty-six convicted murderers in Texas and found that the majority of them had two shared experiences: they grew up in abusive households and they never engaged in play as children (Brown and Vaughan 2009). While this research shows an extreme result, it drives home the crucial role of play not only for children but for our society as a whole.

## YOUR JOURNEY THROUGH THESE PAGES

The PAL model will illuminate the expert you already are and provide you with a way to bridge gaps in understanding so that all well-intended parties can support the ultimate goal—children's growth and learning. A fun tip: I know some of you are like me and are knowledge hoarders. One of the first things this model did for me way back in the day was provide a container in which to put my understanding. When I gleaned a gold nugget from someone or from a book, I'd say, "Okay, so where does this fit? Oh, it's an understanding of what's happening as children are in the environment," for example. This model will give you a structure to categorize your brain research and offer you a science-supported way to communicate about what you know in your heart to be the most developmentally healthy way to nurture children's learning.

You will find Gold Nuggets, Aha Note! and the Practice of the Educator sections in each chapter to help implement the phase's wisdom into your teaching practice. The Gold Nuggets summarize the most important takeaways from the chapter. Aha Note! gives you a life-changing perspective, and the Practice of the Educator offers exercises to bring the ideas from the chapter into practice in your teaching setting.

Additionally, at the conclusion of this book, you'll find a Reader's Guide in appendix A. Within this guide are questions for each chapter designed to inspire discussion and reflection, as well as further applications for your teaching setting. As you conclude each chapter, bring the material to life by spending time with the chapter's questions found in the guide. Doing so will not only give you context for your own setting and teaching practice but also will help you make the absolute most out of the time we'll spend together within the pages of this book.

CHAPTER 2

# THE FOUNDATION

Life in classrooms, after all, is life itself. The learning environment is a complex, living reflection of a teacher's values.
—Bill Ayers

## The Foundation

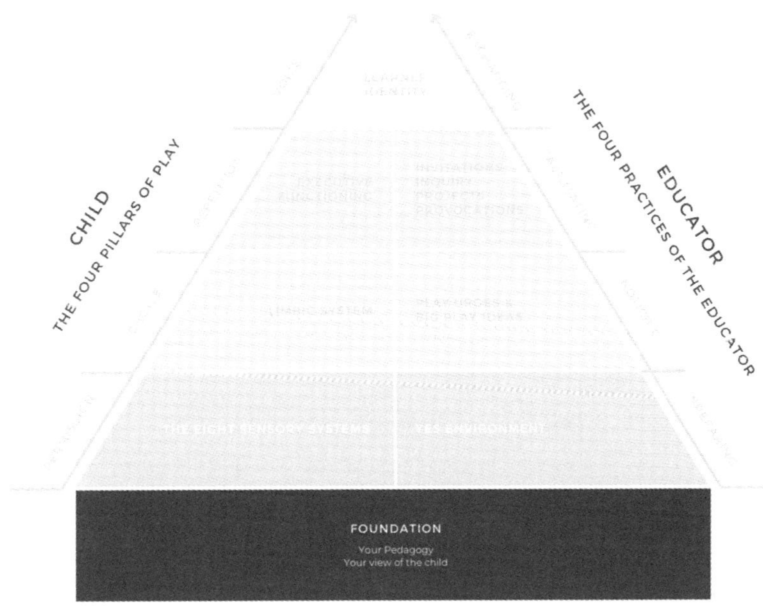


As we enter into more in-depth discussion of the Play-Activated Learning (PAL) model in the following chapters, we'll begin at the beginning—the foundation. In many ways, this is really *your* foundation. The beliefs and views you hold will set the stage and inform your experience with the four pillars, including how you bring this understanding into your play-based practice.

One of the most important moments in my career happened in my first year of teaching kindergarten in a public school. I came to kindergarten with more than ten years of experience with three- and four-year-olds. In my previous school, some people called me "Mary Poppins" because of the lack of behavior issues in my setting.

On the first day of kindergarten, the children arrived, and Corbin, a blond-haired, blue-eyed boy, entered the classroom by punching another child in the cheek. Chaos unfolded immediately.

Where was that Mary Poppins bag of tricks? Nothing I said seemed to settle Corbin's upset. Every day Corbin arrived and chaos was unleashed. Books, tables, chairs, desks. Whatever Corbin could pick up would go flying as he expressed his rage. What was going on? No carpetbag was going to help me with this.

The challenge of Corbin's behavior and its impact on my classroom was soul-crushing to me as an educator. Open play periods became an open nightmare. It was certain that Corbin would become enraged by another student and someone would get hurt.

Four weeks into school and things were not improving. How would I survive this year? I began questioning whether I was cut out for teaching. Should I look for a new job?

Karen, another kindergarten teacher, saw me sitting in my room after school with my hands on my forehead crying. I explained what was going on, including my frustration and deep, heartfelt discouragement. It felt like my classroom was falling apart.

"I use the rainbow system, and it is magic," Karen explained. "I have a yardstick painted with green at the top, and it goes through all the colors to red at the bottom. The children each have their own clip with their name. Everyone starts on green. There are blue, purple, orange, and yellow behaviors, and, of course, red is the note home to the parents."

The next day Karen proudly brought me a rainbow yardstick with clips for each of my students. "I made you the system. My gift."

I put the stick up on my whiteboard and explained it to my students just before recess. "We will begin this when you return from playing outside," I let them know.

Upon returning from recess, Corbin immediately slugged another child in the arm as they entered the room.

The class erupted in yelling, "He is on red! Red! Corbin's on red!"

The entire class watched as I addressed Corbin.

"That's a note home, and put your clip on red," I quietly told Corbin.

The color in his face was flushed as red as the stick. "Who cares?! Nothing matters now—I'm already on red."

I saw it as clear as my own two feet. He felt shamed. I had shamed him.

Brené Brown (2013) defines shame as "the intensely painful feeling or experience of believing that we are flawed and therefore unworthy of love and belonging—something we've experienced, done, or failed to do makes us unworthy of connection."

I took the rainbow system down that day. It was just another version of the red light/green light system. These kinds of behavior paradigms are a product of the assembly line model of education. The whole purpose is to have quiet, compliant children. Shaming is a tool for compliance.

My year with Corbin was one of my most challenging, but I believed in him and his capacity to be his best self. The next year, Corbin came to my classroom on the first day of school.

"Hey Mrs. Haughey, do you want me to take down your chairs?"

"That would be amazing!" I responded as he gave me a side hug.

Nearly every day that year, he would come to my classroom before the first bell, give me a side hug, and take down my chairs. I still cry when I think about it. He knew I believed in him. And every day that he took down those chairs, I knew he believed in me.

## YOUR PEDAGOGY MATTERS

I realized that day that the rainbow stick was not congruent with my personal pedagogy. I think we need to clearly understand our own pedagogy before we jump into the heart of the PAL model. *Pedagogy* is defined by the Merriam-Webster dictionary as the "the art, science, or profession of teaching." It comes from the Greek word *paidagogos*, which is a combination of *paidos* ("child") and *agogos* ("leader").

Our pedagogy, then, is our method and practice of leading children. What is your method and practice? What beliefs do you hold around what your role is? Around the children? The purpose of your setting and its activities? Above all, your pedagogy is how you believe children learn. Everything you are doing right now in your setting is a function of your pedagogy—the way you set up the room, the materials you put in your environment, the structure of your day. Your pedagogy refers to the theory and practice of learning and how this process influences the development of learners. This is the key: the process develops the learner.

Your pedagogy determines how you teach, and it *is* the act of teaching. Your pedagogy determines your actions, judgments, approaches, and strategies. It defines your theory of learning and your understanding of young children and their needs. Your pedagogy describes the behaviors children encounter during the learning process, and it's the framework of how learning works and how you interact with your students.

Most educators have no idea what their pedagogy is. This is often referred to as the "hidden curriculum," a term coined by Phillip Jackson (1990) in his book *Life in Classrooms*, originally published in 1968. Many teachers unquestioningly, and without reflection, accept the belief system or systems that were used to educate and "discipline" them when they were students.

Because you're here, I know that this is not, or is no longer, the case for you.

## THE ASSEMBLY LINE MODEL OF EDUCATION

The current crisis in early childhood education is the pervasive use of the assembly line pedagogy and its damaging impact on the growth and development of young children. This style of pedagogy is more than 150 years old and was inspired, in part, by Horace Mann in 1843. The model was simple: group children together according to their age and have them all taught the same things in the same room by the same teacher.

Sadly, although we've advanced scientifically, technologically, and socially over the past century, our educational environments still look nearly the same as they did a hundred years ago. Children sit in rows listening while the teacher transmits the knowledge.

Seth Godin (2012), in his must-read book *Stop Stealing Dreams (What Is School For?)*, explains that 150 years ago, society became outraged about child labor. There were two outstanding issues. First, children were taking jobs from adults as child labor was considerably cheaper. Second, children were getting injured and being abused in the factories. Compulsory education was sold to the industrialists as a means to develop more compliant workers (Godin 2012).

There is debate around whether the assembly line model was intentionally created to develop a society of people who would do as they were told, or perhaps this cultural development was simply an unintended by-product of this model. But it is clear to me, as well as to many educational theorists, that developing obedient and compliant children is an operative goal of the assembly line model of education (Robinson 2006). A "good" student is a compliant student. Children are to be seen and not heard. They talk only when asked. Fast-forward to today's (relatively unchanged) classroom.

The assembly line paradigm is still influencing our settings deeply. It is widely believed by society at large that

- an effective teacher has a quiet, obedient room;
- an effective teacher has students walking in straight lines without talking; and
- an effective teacher produces compliant children.

For those of us who understand the science behind child-led, play-based teaching as the gold standard of education, this is a chilling scenario. In the assembly line model, it's just another day at school.

## THE FOUR BELIEFS OF THE ASSEMBLY LINE MODEL

The hallmarks of an assembly line model pedagogy include four key beliefs and carry with them some very heavy implications for children and adults alike.

### Belief #1: The Child Is an Empty Vessel

Like a mold on the factory line, a child is seen as a passive participant in the process of education, waiting for the educator to fill them with all they need to be successful in academic learning. The teacher's job is to "pour" the required knowledge into the child so the child can leave as a shiny replica of all the other children who've passed through the system.

As parents, educators, and care providers with an understanding of children's natural developmental processes, we've seen that this is an impossible scenario, and the implications are nothing short of tragic for the many children who must suppress their own ideas, thoughts, and perspectives in favor of allowing themselves to be filled with the "right" kind of knowledge.

These are the assumptions baked into the "child as empty vessel" belief:

- Children should do their work without questioning and with no resistance.
- Obedient children are neat and efficient.
- Children have no say in what they are asked to do and cannot decline participation.
- Children who do resist are considered "failing."

## Belief #2: All Children Have the Same Educational Needs

The damage caused by the belief that children need the same thing at the same time is heartbreaking. Children's needs are approached through the lens of "meeting benchmarks and standards." There is no room for children to follow their own interests in the assembly line paradigm. Instead, they need to be learning according to their age group, and that learning must be demonstrated so that we know everyone is ready to go to the next grade level. It is the idea of a "quality" education through the standardization of learning outcomes. Fast food is standardized and predictable. Yet, just like fast food, the standardization of education is causing more harm than good. Children's growth and development are not linear but rather organic.

Since children are seen as empty vessels, they enter the classroom each year, are fed the requisite facts and information by rote, and are then expected to leave that classroom with the "right" assessment results to show that teaching has been effective.

This means that

- children do the same work at the same time;
- children are educated in "batches" by age; and
- children are taught and measured by standardized curricula.

## Belief #3: Children Who Are Not Meeting Benchmarks Are Failing

Within the assembly line paradigm, children are held to a rigid set of academic standards and milestones typically based on their age and sometimes their assessment scoring. These criteria, and consequently, how children are expected to progress academically, don't consider the developmental processes unfolding, nor do they account for the varying nature of this unfolding within each child.

When children are viewed within a framework of benchmarks, milestones, and standards that don't take development or individuality into account, this creates a dynamic of pressure and shame within the learning setting. Often operating under their *own* pressure and embarrassment imposed by administrators or the academic system at large, educators can unwittingly contribute to this cycle by rewarding those children who "measure up" and calling out those who are "doing it wrong."

This cycle creates an environment of shame and competition based on how children are meeting expectations that are, in most cases, inappropriate and unrealistic given the diverse nature of how they learn and develop. Rather than each child being viewed as a whole, innately brilliant human being, they're viewed as numbers associated with a name, with boxes to be checked—or not.

The value of learning shifts in this context, and it becomes more important to meet these standards than to truly embrace and enjoy the educational process. What could be a flourishing of children's natural wonder and sense of exploration when it comes to academic learning instead becomes a checklist of sorts. In short, children who don't meet benchmarks or check all the appropriate boxes for their age and grade are seen as failing. Sadly, this can become a perspective taken not only by educators and caregivers but by children themselves.

When children feel pressured to meet expectations and then inevitably fail to meet some of these arbitrary markers, the result is personal shame and a culture of competition. Growth is stifled while a fear of failure and "not being enough" is cultivated. Rather than developing their own unique genius and innate intelligence, children are caught up in comparing themselves to others and trying to "win" or feeling shame about their perceived deficiencies—or both.

THE CYCLE OF SHAME & COMPETITION

Over time, the external pressure stemming from the expectations of families and educators can become the internal dialogue of the child. As they internalize the experience of not "fitting" within the parameters of the system or meeting developmental expectations, children are at risk for developing a fierce inner critic, one that may likely inhibit their motivation to try new things and cut down on their receptiveness to learning opportunities. Simply put, when faced with the choice of not being enough, yet again, it becomes safer not to try at all.

### Belief #4: Success Means Meeting Milestones on Time or Earlier

In the assembly line model, time is of the essence. As with a factory belt that must keep churning along at a certain speed so that all its products turn out identically and on time, children are seen as needing to keep pace with arbitrary markers that are not based in the science of learning.

The sooner a child walks, the better.
The sooner a child talks, the better.
The sooner a child is potty trained, the better.
The sooner a child knows the alphabet, the better.
The sooner a child reads, the better.

As my friend Rae Pica calls it—the "earlier is better" culture leads to a dynamic that is counter to learning and growth. For decades, families have been indoctrinated to believe that their children should be achieving certain milestones based on their age. This has damaging, and sometimes even devastating, effects on both parents and children. For example, as a young mother, I was asked if my baby was crawling. My children were late crawlers and walkers, and friends and family would comment that *their* children crawled or walked much earlier. This left me wondering whether I was doing something wrong. Parents feel pressured that their children should be hitting milestones sooner rather than later.

Parenthood can be challenging. Adding the pressure of age-based milestones affects parents in untold ways (and can have an obvious trickle-down effect on their children too).

## OUR ROLE IN EFFECTING CHANGE

When we look at the roots of the assembly line model of education, we see that it was based on an outdated belief that society would be better off if everyone was in lockstep. We must acknowledge that we have all been subject to it in one way or another and come to understand how it has affected early childhood education.

Our current education system has been failing young children for decades. In fact, it failed my own son.

One day in 1989, I walked into my son's kindergarten classroom. It was an unremarkable setting with an orderly block center, a place for dramatic play, and a very overwhelming computer area. Schools were using Macintosh computers that were big enough to hurt someone if they tipped over. Earlier that day, I had received a call from his teacher, telling me she needed to talk to me immediately.

"Mrs. Haughey, thank you for coming." Mrs. Jones, his teacher, stood in front of me with pumps, hose, and an outfit that could have come from the 1950s.

I took a seat next to her, and she pulled out a folder full of his work.

"Mrs. Haughey, I am very concerned about Ben." She opened the file and showed me one worksheet after another. "Your son can't sit still. He falls out of his seat. And when I tell him to get up and get back in his chair—he cries and cries. He is not ready for first grade. He can't trace. He can't stay in the lines. He can't sit still. He can't take my correction."

My mouth must have hit my chest. I was floored. He knew the alphabet and sounds; he could count to one hundred. He was ready. How would he feel with his friends going on to first grade while he was staying behind?

"It doesn't matter what he knows if he can't do what he is told. If he can't follow the rules and write in the lines, he can't move on."

That day I withdrew my son from that school and sent him to the backyard to play.

The moment my son went out to play was the moment Fairy Dust Teaching/Wunderled (my websites) were born.

The idea that his compliance was more important than his love of learning set the fire in my belly that has brought me here today. And guess what? My son graduated in the top 5 percent of his high school class. While talking about this means I'm participating in the same system of measurement used by the assembly line paradigm, I find it ironic that a child who at one time "didn't measure up" went on to excel academically in this context.

There is a parasite feeding on our educational system, and it is the idea that children are little sponges that we can mold and shape to our liking. That day I put a stake in the ground not only for my own child but for every child I could possibly affect. I've done this through my own practice, as well as by reaching as many early childhood educators as possible through Fairy Dust Teaching/Wunderled. Your presence here is not only welcome, my friend, but crucial to the well-being and healthy development of children around the world.

It is time to recognize that the assembly line paradigm has a distinct, recognizable pattern: everything is outcome driven. Its underpinnings foster competition and shame, with children simply the products of a system of outcomes. Children who succeed according to standards can be seen as superior by their teachers and parents. Meanwhile the sense of competition and pressure never let up, and those children who are not seen as successful can spend a lifetime doubting their own worth. Parents often feel judged as inadequate when their child does not meet the expectations of the school system.

Educators, too, have been negatively affected for multiple decades. They are expected to have all the children in their class meet or exceed benchmarks. Families expect "school readiness." Educators who "prepare" children can become the "favorite" among parents, thus feeding the same sense of competition and pressure among their peers that they felt as children.

The cycle must end. And we are the ones who can do it.

By arming yourself with the brain science of play and developing the skills and confidence to powerfully demonstrate why play is the gold standard in education, you can make a difference not only in the lives of the children in your care but in the future of our world.

## OUR VIEW OF THE CHILD

One of the most important steps in moving away from the assembly line paradigm is to clearly define our view of the child, thus its foundational role in the PAL model. In 1994 Loris Malaguzzi, founder of the Reggio Emilia approach, wrote a groundbreaking article, "Your Image of the Child: Where Teaching Begins." In this article, he asserts that it is your "image of the child that directs you as you . . . relate to a child" (52–56).

It's important to uncover the views we hold that we don't realize are blocking our capacity to see the child in front of us. Imagine that these undiscovered and unknown views are like looking through a dirty window.

Unpacking our views of the child is an experience like the woman looking out her window in Paulo Coelho's story "The Dirty Laundry":

A newlywed couple settled into their new home. Each morning at breakfast, the wife observed their neighbor hanging laundry and commented critically on its cleanliness, suggesting the neighbor lacked washing skills or needed better detergent. Her husband listened quietly. This continued for weeks. One day the wife saw the neighbor's laundry was clean and wondered aloud, "Who finally taught her to wash correctly?" Her husband revealed that he had cleaned their own windows that morning.

Instead of having cloudy vision, educators must truly seek to see and understand each child for who they are, rather than come to the learning environment with preconceived ideas and beliefs that may ascribe certain characteristics that aren't there to children. There is beautifully unique depth, complexity, and wonder inside each young human we encounter.

Each of us wants to be understood, and children are no different. When someone makes an assumption about us, we don't feel seen, and we certainly don't feel connected to that person. For educators to have the greatest impact, they need to examine their beliefs and open space to genuinely see, hear, and understand children.

In his Education Hub article "Image of the Child," educator Daniel Whitaker (2020) shares some common ways we limit children with our views. I have expanded his list to five limiting views of the child that exist in our culture, the most common limiting views that affect the learning environment.

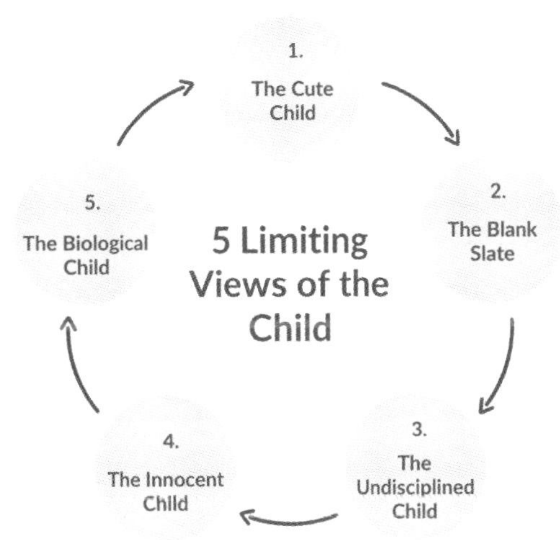


## The Cute Child

"Isn't that cute?" You'll hear that a lot if you spend any time around young children. This view primarily sees young child as cute, and it values the adorable and charming things children say and do. I can't count how many times I have heard another educator say, "He said the cutest thing."

This became a glaring issue for me during my short run giving children's sermons on Sundays at the church where I worked in the early 2000s. The congregation would laugh when the children said something "cute." It made the hair stand up on my head because it felt so disrespectful. These children were sharing their honest ideas and thoughts about the topic. And what do they get in response? An entire room of adults laughing. It was so wrong. Did the congregation view children as entertainment? Were the children there to delight and tickle people's cute buttons? Not on my watch. Yet unable to force change, I did not stay in that position.

In essence, when we view children's personalities and actions as cute, we aren't valuing the person. It sends the message that a child's worth is found in an adult's entertainment. It even assumes children don't have feelings, or we wouldn't laugh at them.

Some implications of this worldview we see in the classroom include

- decorating children's rooms and settings with cute and endearing decorations and materials;
- asking questions that will elicit "cute" responses; and
- expecting children to be sweet, quiet, happy, and charming all the time.

## The Blank Slate

Like me, maybe you've also experienced this next dynamic at play. I had this underlying feeling I could help *any* child adjust and adapt to my classroom. There was no child I couldn't bring into my community, I told myself. Sounds great . . . but it implies that I control the children's responses. When Corbin had outbursts, I thought if I could only say the right thing, he would calm down and integrate into the community, as if he were a programmable robot.

The image of the child as an empty vessel or blank slate dates to seventeenth-century philosopher John Locke, who asserted the child's mind at birth is without ideas. Locke called this a *tabula rasa*, or a blank slate (Ezell 1983).

According to this view, a child's mind requires an adult to fill it with information. Children are viewed as malleable and trainable. The image of the child as an empty vessel is seen in curriculum choices that fill the child up with academic "basics" like the alphabet and numbers. This image assumes that children don't have anything to contribute to the learning process.

When we approach young children as needing preparation for elementary school, we remove them from the process of learning. They become passive recipients, with following instructions and obedience as their only contributions.

This lens of children came into focus for me when I conducted my first preassessment before the start of my universal pre-K class. Every child was assessed for their existing knowledge. Clearly, the goal of the preassessment was to provide documentation of how much of the curriculum was already present in my class of twenty little blank slates. The intended goal, in my estimation, was to provide a checklist of sorts that would inform the administration and me of what the children may be "missing" and what I would need to "teach to" with my curriculum. It was infuriating to me that the curriculum was based on filling children with the academic basics and not on what would actually be beneficial to their growth. It felt as though a line was being drawn in the sand between things like reading and basic mathematics—and the crucial play-based fundamentals that would lay the optimal foundation for learning them, like sensory exploration and process-oriented activities.

These are some implications of this worldview that we see in the classroom:

- Expecting complete obedience
- At circle time, using rote methods to teach the alphabet, counting, sight words, and more, with the goal of drilling in the basics
- Using worksheets for practicing rote skills on paper as a means to embed them in the child's memory
- Featuring wall posters showing the knowledge the teacher is working to fill the children with

## The Undisciplined Child

Corbin entered my classroom with clear issues regarding how he processed his experience of the other children. Surely I could adjust his nervous system—right?! All he needed was a little "training."

The image of the child as needing discipline holds the belief that a child is some kind of wild animal that needs to be tamed and domesticated. Discipline is seen as an essential part of training children to be a part of society. This perspective was influenced by eighteenth-century theologian John Wesley, the founder of Methodism. Children are viewed as inferior to adults and require strict discipline. He is quoted as saying, "Break their will, that you may save their soul" (Heitzenrater 2001, 279).

This heartbreaking perspective views children's behavior as "manipulation" and "control." The crying baby is just manipulating the mother to pick her up. The two-year-old's meltdown is just an attempt to control the adults in the room. The child is "spoiled." It implies some kind of willful, malicious intent on the part of children.

One year when I taught three-year-olds, one of the children would cry when her mother dropped her off. She would cling to her mother and beg her to stay. My coteacher would roll her eyes and whisper to me, "She is doing that to make her mother feel bad." Maria was a shy and nervous child. Her mother was her safe place. It was shocking to me that her needs were labeled as a manipulation and that this was a primary way someone would understand and explain her behavior.

Here are some implications of this worldview we see in the classroom:

- Giving bribes and rewards for desired behaviors
- Believing that children should obey all adults' commands
- Expecting that children should walk the school hallways in straight lines and be completely silent
- Saying things like "yes, sir" and "no, ma'am" to adults as a sign of respect
- Not allowing upset behavior in the classroom. Children are expected to contain their feelings and emotions
- Using time-out chairs and removing recess as corrective measures

## The Innocent Child

The image of the child as innocent holds childhood as a special paradise that must be protected from corruption. This well-intended image of the child is constructed through adults' sentimental and idealistic attachment to childhood.

The idea of innocence holds young children as pure and unspoiled by society's evils. Many of us look back at our own childhoods with eyes of idealism, seeing it as a carefree time without worry. As a young mother, I wanted my children to have a childhood of innocence.

This idea of childhood's innocence was brought to light by the eighteenth-century thinker Jean-Jacques Rousseau. Rousseau believed children were born guiltless, and through life's experiences, they learn what he called "disagreeableness" (Cleverley and Phillips 1987). This view brought forth the idea that children needed to be protected and shielded from the evils of life.

Perceiving children as innocent demands that we protect children from the evil in the world. Adults care for the "garden of childhood" and carefully select what the children can be exposed to, removing the questionable. The children don't have a voice in what is in their best interests. Instead, it is the job of their protectors, the adults. Children are looked upon as vulnerable and helpless. In this dynamic, they are not empowered to find or use their voices and are regarded as incapable of expressing their needs.

I am still moved by the incredible conversations I had with my pre-K class the day I heard that someone dear to my family had died unexpectedly. I sat down with the children and said, "I am very sad. I just heard that someone very important to my family has died." Immediately, the children started sharing their own losses: "I lost my grandpa." "Our dog, Chip, died." A child even shared the loss of a beloved blanket. Children are capable of deep conversations and profound reflections when we approach difficult topics with developmental appropriateness.

These are some implications of this worldview we see in the classroom:

- Viewing children as helpless; you often hear adults talking about children in front of them as if they have no feelings
- Doing the basic activities of life for the child, like serving food, picking up clothes, and so forth, when the child has the competency to start doing them for themselves
- Not talking about important life occurrences because of a worry that it might be too much for the child
- Censoring materials and books to remove those that don't hold idealistic views
- Keeping children safe by not allowing risky play

## The Biological Child

The final image of the child is biological. This view holds the expectation that children will accomplish typical milestones at the "normal stage" of development, as compared to children of the same chronological age. This image of the young child has families and teachers striving to have all children achieve or exceed the expected milestones of their age. In the last thirty years, I've seen an emphasis in our culture that the sooner a child reaches these milestones, like crawling, walking, and talking, the better. This has put pressure on parents to push their child's development—pressure that distracts from celebrating the beautiful, natural unfolding of the personality and humanity of the child.

Here are some implications of this worldview we see in the classroom:

- Judging children on their size as compared to their peers
- Expecting all children to have the same capacities at the same time

Take time in the next week to listen for these five views in the conversations of families, colleagues, and administrators.

- Which view is more prominent in your community?
- How are these views affecting decision-making?
- How might these views be affecting children's behavior?

## GOLD NUGGETS

- Your beliefs and views about teaching young children form the foundation of your approach to play-based learning. It's important to understand your own pedagogy, which is your method and practice of leading children.
- The current crisis in early childhood education stems from the outdated assembly line model of education, which focuses on compliance, standardization, and arbitrary age-based milestones. This model can be damaging to children's growth and development.
- To move away from this model, we must examine our views of children. We often have limiting beliefs about children that we aren't aware of, which cloud how we see and relate to them.

## THE PRACTICE OF THE EDUCATOR: THE FOUNDATION

A powerful step in the process of revolutionizing how we relate to and teach children—and therefore nurture their brilliance—is to take a look at your own view of the child. In the following exercise, look at four perspectives of the view of the child. The best way to approach this reflection is to write down your first thought—don't overthink it. It's often the automatic answer that holds the truth. Ideally, this exercise should take anywhere from fifteen to thirty minutes.

> *Aha Note!*
>
> Everything you are doing right now in your setting is a function of your pedagogy.

These are the same prompts I have given students in my Wunderled Certification, a yearlong study program. Answering these questions is life-changing. I have had educators break down crying, telling me that for the first time they felt closer to who they really are as an educator. This is a process that is designed to give you massive insight and transformation, and I hope it will inspire just that for you.

The four facets you are going to unpack include the following:

- Inherited: These come from your own childhood and family.
- Personal: This is your own personal view.
- Economic/political: This reflects the economic and political climate around children.
- Cultural: This springs from the culture around children, specific to where you teach.

It's an eye-opening exercise to reflect on the view of the child through the language we use. I want you to think about how people talk to children as you move through the prompts.

### Inherited View

Our past affects how we see the world. We inherit the stories, ideas, and perspectives of those who came before us. Through messages that have been passed on through generations, our families directly influence what we have come to believe. As a result, these messages have shaped the lens through which we view the world. Reflect on your childhood and family. Tap into the voice of the child within that context.

- In your family, how were children disciplined for misbehavior? What kind of language was used?
- When a situation arose that rendered a choice you made as misbehavior, was your story or opinion about the matter considered important? Why or why not? Did you have a voice? Did anyone listen to you?
- As a child, if you went to your parents to ask for supplies to build a cool idea you had, what would be their response? Would they provide what you were asking for? Why or why not?
- What was the primary pressure you felt from your parents as it pertained to school?

### *DISTILL IT!*

Summarize the general inherited view of the child held by your family. Restate it as a belief about the voices of children.

BELIEF ⟶ ____________________________________

## Personal View

Our view of the child matters. It affects our interactions, communication, decisions, and perspective of the child. Reflect on your personal view of the child. Consider their voice, the perspectives they hold, and the value you place on them as human beings.

- Thinking about your "why," expand on the reasons you've chosen to educate children. What is your role in this relationship? What is the role of the child?
- Looking back on your teaching history and your relationship with children, what, if any, behaviors from children have you found to be intolerable? In such cases, what made these behaviors intolerable? If there are none, why do you think this is the case? Remember, only you will see your reflections. Be honest with yourself.
- Make a list of every opportunity you give to children to foster a sense of independence, self-management, and autonomy within the context of your learning environment. Consider opportunities indoors and outdoors where

their voices are trusted and heard. It's also valuable to consider the cultural implications of this in your region. How are a sense of independence, self-management, and autonomy in children viewed and prioritized? How can you honor and support this within your learning environment?

- Is there a primary pressure you place on children in your care? Consider what you expect of them. One way to pinpoint this is to think about the things that make you feel nervous, worried, fearful, or angry.

### *DISTILL IT!*

Summarize your personal view of the child's voice within the context of your learning environment.

Restate it as a belief.

BELIEF ⟶ ____________________________

## Economic/Political View

Consider the powerful impact economics and politics have on people's lives. Reflect on how the political and economic climate affects children. Think about how the language used through political and economic channels reveals commonly held beliefs about the view of the child.

- Do you feel your country or government trusts children? If yes, where does the evidence lie? If not, what evidence supports your opinion?
- As you reflect on the most recent political campaigns in your country, what messages are communicated about the view of the child and each of their educational needs? What do these messages imply about children?
- What economic or political pressure do you see being imposed on children?

### *DISTILL IT!*

Summarize the impact of the economic/political climate on your country's view of the child.

Restate it as a belief society holds.

BELIEF ⟶ ____________________________

## Cultural View

Culture has an enormous influence on children. Everything they see, hear, encounter, and learn is embedded in deeply held cultural beliefs, languages, traditions, and customs. Reflect on the impact of the culture in your context as you consider the implications culture holds for the children in your care. In this sense, we're thinking about culture less in the context of language and customs but, rather, the culture's predominant image of the child. Consider the kinds of statements you hear that are shared daily with children.

- As you reflect on your context, what is the number one complaint about children that you hear? What does this belief say about children's competencies?
- As children navigate their day, what is the typical classroom management method used in your setting?
- In your context, how often are children empowered to embrace opportunities to make decisions about their day? Do you feel you are in a child-led or a teacher-led learning environment? How do you know?
- As you reflect on your setting, what is the number one behavioral expectation placed on children?

### *DISTILL IT!*

Summarize the overall cultural view of the child in your country.

Restate it as a belief.

BELIEF ⟶ ______________________________

## The Language We Use

After you complete this reflection surrounding views of the child, consider the many ways we speak to children. Did you know, according to early childhood educator Tom Drummond, that up to 80 percent of what adults say to children is a command statement? In a Fairy Dust Teaching conference workshop, Tom said this: "Command statements are a type of pushy statement. These statements include directives (e.g., "Throw the ball"), tutorials (e.g., "What color is this?"), and queries (e.g., "Do you want more milk?") (Drummond, 2020) On his website, www.tomdrummond.com, Tom explains his "function coding" of conversations with children through two kinds of statements adults make: informational and directive. He discovered that "the most effective teachers I know habitually speak to their children with *informational* **percentages above 60%.**" What follows is inspired by Drummond's work and conversations. I highly recommend reading his website and articles on conversations with children. See appendix B, Observation of the Statements You Use with Children, page 152, for a helpful framework for examining what you say to children.

**Commanding/Directing:** These statements direct or order a child to do something.

- "Sit with your hands in your lap."
- "Walk without talking."
- "Finish your work."

**Punishing/Threatening:** These statements imply or explicitly state a consequence for a child's behavior. "If you act like this, then you will not be able to play here."

- "If you don't finish your lunch, you can't have your dessert."

**Discounting/Dismissing:** These statements minimize or invalidate a child's feelings, thoughts, or experiences.

- "Are you sure that's the truth? We will have to look further."
- "Don't be silly; that couldn't have hurt."

**Shaming/Belittling:** Statements that criticize, belittle, or humiliate a child.

- "I have told you a hundred times, don't put the paint in the dramatic play center. What am I going to do with you?"
- "You're such a messy child."
- "You're so careless; look at the mess you made."

**Informational/Explanatory:** These statements provide factual information or explanations.

- "Today we are baking bread."
- "We need to wear our coats because it's cold outside."
- "The playground is closed due to rain."

**Validating/Affirming:** Statements that acknowledge and accept a child's feelings or experiences.

- "It's okay to be sad; everyone feels sad sometimes."
- "It's okay to make mistakes; we can learn from them."
- "I can see you have worked hard on cleaning up your area."

**Questioning/Inquiring:** These statements seek information or encourage critical thinking. They can be open-ended or closed-ended.

- "Where would you like to play today?"
- "What do you think will happen if we mix these colors?"
- "Are you ready to go?"

A final tip: Consider recording your conversations with children. It's interesting to hear our automatic statements to children. In my own practice, seeing and hearing my actions and words with children had a dramatic impact. While this list is partial, it is a great start to becoming aware of how we talk to children.

# CHAPTER 3

# PERMISSION

Childhood play leads to a lot of sensory integration as the child organizes the sensations of his body and gravity, along with sight and sound.
—A. Jean Ayres

## Permission Pillar

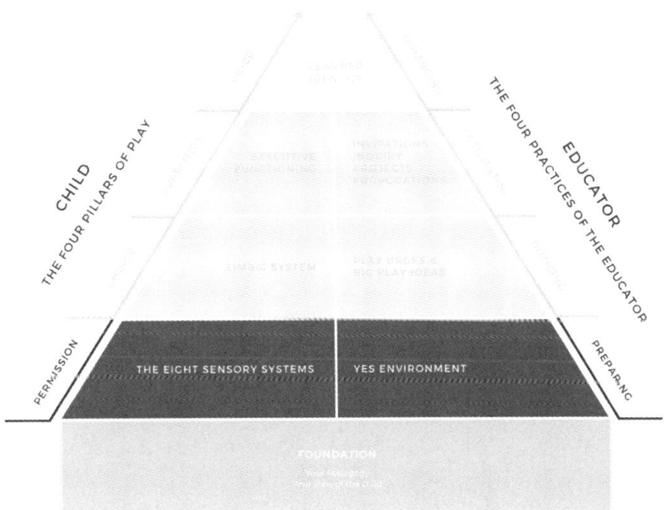


As we continue with the Play-Activated Learning (PAL) model, we move forward from the foundation of our own perspective and understanding and shift deeper into the child's. The Permission phase considers how children interface with their environment with one of the greatest, most awe-inspiring gifts we were all given at birth—the sensory systems. Our task during this phase is to prepare an environment that gives permission to children's sensory growth and development.

In 2013 I was hired to teach a class of three-year-olds. The children's behaviors were so out of control that two other educators had left. When I arrived for my first day, I perceived an absence of richness in texture and materials in the room. I saw few materials, and the environment felt sterile and barren. I spent the first week observing the children and making plans based on their needs, interests, and social climate.

One of the first things I noticed was the children's love of transporting materials from one place to another. In other words, these children were experts at scattering and dumping things everywhere. When it was time to pick up, the floors were covered in play materials and the children resisted helping. How could I address this need, this play schema, to transport and dump? How could I create an environment of permission for this schema? A play schema is a behavior or action repeated by the child during play through which they explore the world around them. This is a way they bring understanding to their experiences and is a natural part of their learning and development. On a physical level, I saw within the children a strong need for movement in the actions of carrying and transporting. What would happen if I put out containers of all kinds? Would the children seize the opportunity to incorporate them into their transportation of the materials? Thinking about the sensory experience, I wondered what would happen if those containers were in various textures: woven baskets, leather bags, steel buckets, plastic shopping baskets, even fabric purses.

Filled with inspiration and energized by the aha moment I'd had, I went searching for containers in local thrift shops. I found metal buckets in three sizes, upcycled totes woven from candy wrappers, boxes with lids made of various materials, and sturdy shopping totes from the grocery store. The next day, I placed fifteen empty containers around the room in every area of the environment.

Immediately the children found the containers. What floored me about the addition of these containers was how it elevated their play to an entirely new level. Before adding them, the children's play was of a destructive nature. Their energy seemed focused on eradicating what was in front of them. Once the carrying containers were added to the room, their play exploded in creativity! For example, a group of children created a bus out of blocks and chairs. They boarded the bus with their bags packed, ready to "ride home." Before I introduced the containers, all I had witnessed was the children transporting and dumping materials everywhere. It felt like frenzied, frenetic chaos that had suddenly shifted to wonder and creation.

A very welcome additional aspect of this new dynamic was that I could engage the children in picking up by incorporating the carrying containers. "Who will fill this basket with all the blocks?" I would start the cleaning up process with plenty of time, so there was no rush or pressure. As I reflected on the environment, I discerned that the previous teacher had hoped to reduce the destruction and her cleanup work by keeping the environment to a bare minimum of elements, but this only furthered the children's frustration as their needs were not being met. They needed sensory-rich and intentional materials that satisfied more than just their visual and auditory senses. The new carrying containers addressed their sense of movement and opened up a pathway for creativity and exploration. It gave them permission.

I adopted a neutral and earthy palette of colors in the room that gave a calm and soothing feeling. Within the new palette's soft colors, the materials stood out with varied textures.

Those children were providing me with firsthand, anecdotal evidence for what I knew in my core: sensory processing is the starting point of any early childhood learning environment. In fact, the greater the range of sensory input, the more effect it has on physiological activity and brain growth. And with this, we arrive at the entry point of the PAL model: preparing the sensory-rich yes environment.

## HOW THE SENSORY SYSTEM WORKS

The sensory system is the doorway to learning for young children. Children receive information about the world around them through the sensory receptors that then transmit the incoming input to the brain. Think of these sensory neurons as eager receptors waiting to take in the impressions of the surrounding environment.

Understanding the role of sensory systems in young children's development and learning how to support this growth through our classroom environments will provide a foundation for all of our teaching efforts. This understanding becomes our framework and informs how we work with and support children in our setting, from the ways in which we set up our teaching environments to the modalities we use and their timing and structure. A. Jean Ayres, a famous American occupational therapist and author of *Sensory Integration and the Child*, suggested that we consider sensations as nourishment for the brain. The outside world is processed through the children's sensory systems, and the incoming data is like water flowing through streams, the water being electrical impulses. And where does it go? Into the brain, where it is processed into new understandings. Ayres, who also coined the term *sensory integration*, asserted that 90 percent of the brain's activity is processing sensory input (Ayres 2005). With such a vast amount of children's internal energy being spent in this fashion, sensory input clearly deserves and requires our attention.

Our environments provide a palette of sensory experiences. In many ways, this is the tangible curriculum for the child. Not all sensory experiences are equal, and this is where the current problem of our early childhood environments begins. Going back to those eager receptors mentioned previously, children's sensory neurons are like very thirsty, parched participants in this process, and every rich experience is like a pool of nourishing water, filling them with incredible data and intelligence.

Children take in incredible amounts of sensory information about the environment through their sense receptors. However, most of the sensory input in a traditional early childhood setting is visual and auditory. Furthermore, the sensory environments of these settings are what Susan Kovalik (2001), author of *Exceeding Expectations*, calls "secondhand." She explains that secondhand input can be considered representational input. For example, a plastic flower represents a real flower. A flower also can be represented by a video or a book about flowers. These experiences of "flower" lack the multisensory nature of the actual flower. The sensory experience of the natural flower not only activates more of the children's senses but also is more likely to go into their long-term memory. There is simply more depth and richness for the child to engage with and integrate.

Each sensory system sends signals to the brain based on the incoming data, and the child's brain interprets these signals and comes up with a response. To do this, the brain often combines data from multiple sensory systems, which is why we call it sensory integration. The scientific data is clear. The groundwork for higher cognitive and social/emotional abilities lies in well-organized sensory processing (Diamond 2013). Yet most early childhood settings aren't constructed on this truth. We know that when the brain effectively interprets inputs such as pressure, movement, temperature, and stimuli within our sensory systems, it builds the foundation for regulating our nervous systems (Kranowitz 2022). It is when we, as educators and caregivers, keep this interpretation and foundation in mind, that we can best facilitate an environment that creates permission for children's sensory growth and development.

Put simply, in the Permission phase, sensory integration is the base that prepares young children for success in school. It does this by providing them with the capacity to manage their bodies while sitting, the ability to process the educator's instructions, and more.

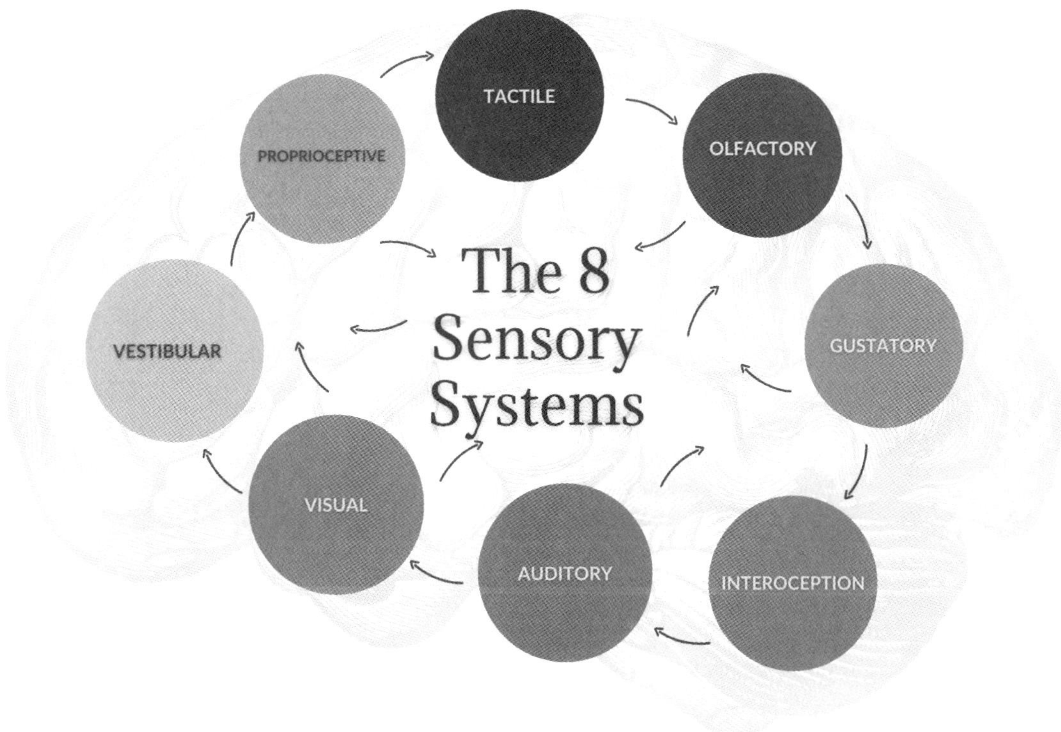


## THE EIGHT SENSORY SYSTEMS

The first stage of the PAL model takes place when the child enters the yes environment we have prepared and begins processing the sensory information there. Experts debate how many senses we have because the sensory cells trigger so many different signals and responses. Rudolph Steiner, founder of Waldorf education, described twelve senses and asserted that certain senses were more important at various stages of development (Steiner 1995). Bob Samples (1987) wrote about nineteen senses that considered the complexity of our sensory cells and responses. The eight sensory systems we will use in this book is a popular model inspired by Ayres's work. It asserts five outward-facing sensory systems: visual, auditory, olfactory (smell), gustatory (taste), and tactile; and three internal sensory systems: vestibular, proprioception, and interoception. Let's look at how we can prepare an environment of permission for each of the eight sensory systems.

| ARISTOTLE'S FIVE SENSES | STEINER'S TWELVE SENSES | SAMPLES'S NINETEEN SENSES | EIGHT SENSORY SYSTEMS |
|---|---|---|---|
| Sight | Life Sense | Sight | Visual System |
| Hearing | Sense of Movement | Hearing | Auditory System |
| Smell | Sense of Balance | Touch | Olfactory System |
| Touch | Sense of Touch | Taste | Gustatory System |
| Taste | Sense of Smell | Smell | Tactile System |
| | Sense of Taste | Balance | Vestibular System |
| | Sense of Sight | Vestibular | Proprioceptive System |
| | Sense of Warmth | Temperature | Interoception |
| | Sense of Hearing | Pain | |
| | Word Sense | Eidetic Imagery | |
| | Sense of Thought | Magnetic | |
| | Ego Sense | Infrared | |
| | | Ultraviolet | |
| | | Ionic | |
| | | Vomeronasal | |
| | | Proximal | |
| | | Electrical | |
| | | Barometric | |
| | | Geogravimetric | |

## THE TACTILE SYSTEM (SENSE OF TOUCH)

On the most basic level, the tactile system helps us define what is self and not self. It is through touch that we find our separateness and our relatedness. Our skin defines the boundary of our self, and it is the primary sensory organ for the tactile system.

### Touch in Our Language

We talk about "thin-skinned" people, being "tough," and being "touched" by an experience. When something is difficult, a child says "'I can't do it; it's too hard."

We use these specific qualities of the sense of touch to describe our relationships. In essence, touch is at the core of our very being. Other examples include "soft-hearted," "rough around the edges," "hotheaded," and "cool under pressure."

## The Physiology of Touch

The skin is the largest organ of the body, with thousands of sensory cells (nerve endings) that detect stimuli such as pressure, weight, temperature, and pain. Our tactile sense enables us to discern the difference between varying textures and surfaces (such as hard/soft, bumpy/smooth). When you touch an apple, your fingertips receive information about its physical qualities—nerve endings are more concentrated in our fingertips than just about any other body part. When you sit, lie down, or run, the tactile sense conveys the quality of that experience—hard, soft, warm, cool, and so forth. Touch also releases the hormone oxytocin, which is calming.

## The Role of Touch in Development

The tactile sense could be called the sense of trust. It is through the sense of touch that we learn to trust (or mistrust) the world. When you consider it more closely, touch is twofold: separating and connecting. Touch is one of the most important components of bonding with another person, and loving touch from others is necessary for an individual's healthy development. This isn't surprising, given that the sense of touch develops in the embryonic state before all the other senses. Touch is a primal sense with the contractions of labor as the infant moves through the birth canal and pressure is applied against the skin. It's the fundamental way in which infants learn about their environment and bond with other people. Think of how we calm crying newborns by holding them closely. The experience of being held and stroked as an infant is critical to healthy growth. Consider the fact that by the time a child reaches one year of age, they have already experienced thousands of tactile interactions that have shaped their trust, learning, and sense of self.

## Educational Implications

Think about the difference between a worksheet about apples versus an actual apple. The fingertips can't feel the physical properties of an apple through a worksheet. In the late 1990s, I heard Joseph Chilton-Pearce, author of several books on human and child development, speak at a conference where he said that the fingers are the "ten hearts" and that the heart is the eleventh finger (Chilton-Pearce 1998). This points to the powerful impact of what our children touch, and it so deeply correlates with making meaningful connections. The current trend of imposing early academics and the heavy use of worksheets frightens me when we consider this in the context of touch. There's a reason that early childhood is play-based: it is touch-based. Children love experiencing the world through their sense of touch—it's how they learn the world.

## Quick Permission Tips: The Tactile System in Your Setting

The child entering our environment is entering through the tactile sense. In that context, educating children in a way that provides them with a secure sense of touch is of utmost importance. Healthy touch gives the growing child a sense of security and builds self-esteem.

The experience of touch in the environment is embodied in subtle experiences like touching wood versus plastic. Providing as natural an environment as possible with real cotton, silk, wood, beeswax, glass, metal, and handmade items offers children a rich palette of touch and an opportunity for sensory exploration. This truth in materials (such as natural wood versus plastic) inspires a child's sense of awe, wonder, and respect.

Consider the following methods for simple yet very meaningful ways to provide a nurturing sensory experience in your classroom or setting:

- Find natural and healthy points of meaningful touch in the room. I stand at the door each morning to greet each student and give them a pat or hug depending on their lead, always letting them choose which one. The most important thing is that they receive a loving, joyful touch of welcome that communicates, "I'm so happy you're here!"
- When we wash our hands or use sanitizer, I hold children's hands with gentle kindness as I give them the soap. I intentionally bring loving kindness to these small gestures to provide a deep sense of safety.
- Children don't have many opportunities to learn how to touch appropriately—we're living in a society fearful of touch. We can

improve on this by dancing and doing circle games and other activities that require hand-holding.

- When a child hurts another child, it's deeply healing for them to lovingly touch the child who has been hurt. This is far more powerful than the standard "I'm sorry." One of my Waldorf mentors guided me to use a healing basket with a boo-boo bunny (ice pack) made out of a washcloth. The children loved it.
- I strive to provide a wide range of textures and surfaces in the environment for centers, art projects, and exploration. These help educate the ever-deepening sense of touch and give children a deep sense of comfort within the process of learning.
- Providing experiences like kneading playdough and squishing clay help educate the sense of touch.

## Addressing Sensory Issues

Children with tactile problems can be touch-sensitive (avoiding touch) or hyposensitive (seeking touch). A rich touch environment can help these children.

- It's important not to touch the back of children who are tactile defensive, as this can be extremely upsetting for them.
- Children who are nervous need to be held tightly to feel the boundary of self. You may notice these children need more hugs throughout the day.
- Remember, touch releases the calming hormone oxytocin. Find out how a child needs tactile support: do they prefer a hug, a pat, or a gentle touch to the hand?
- Rhythmic touch helps reduce anxiety and depression (think of the hand-clapping games that children love to play).
- For touch-seeking children: Consider creating a "sensory corner" with items like weighted blankets or textured toys.

There is so much to be said about the sense of touch. The tactile sense is foundational not only to academic success but also to being a healthy human being.

# THE PROPRIOCEPTIVE SYSTEM (SENSE OF MOVEMENT)

Proprioception is the spatial orientation of one's body within its surroundings. One way I like to think about proprioception is that it's like our body's GPS. It's how we sense where our body parts are and how they move, even without looking. It also helps us understand the movements happening around us.

## Proprioception in Our Language

It's been said that the sense of movement is the mother of joy. "That moved me deeply" and "I was moved to tears" bring this to mind. Think of a very joyful kindergartener. What do they do naturally? They skip!

Our sense of movement and body position has shaped a rich vocabulary of expressions that capture things like emotional states, personal progress, and life challenges: "She carries herself well," "You just have to roll with the punches," "Lean into the challenge," and "I was thrown off course," for example.

## The Physiology of Proprioception

The proprioceptive receptors are found within the muscles, joints, tendons, and ligaments. The organ for the sense of proprioception is the motor nerve system of the spinal cord and the central part of the brain. Twenty pairs of nerves emerge from each side of the spine to give us the sense of movement. This also includes the movement of the eyes, head, neck, and upper trunk.

The ability to proprioceptively perceive one's trunk and limbs is called spatial awareness. This is an awareness of the body in three-dimensional space (that is, forward, backward, up, down, left, and right).

On a deeper level, the sense of proprioception is connected to rhythm—the rhythmic movement of contraction and relaxation, the shortening and lengthening of muscles, the movement from one activity to the next, the flow of how we move through our days, and the movement from one place to another. It's rising to meet the day and resting as we fall asleep. Rhythm is taking space and turning it into time.

## The Role of Proprioception in Development

Proprioception is not only about sensing our own body, its movements, and its orientation. It's also about the movements happening around us in relation to our bodies. For example, when I took over a class of three-year-olds, I noticed they had difficulty during transitions like cleanup time, during which the children's movements became chaotic. They had challenges following along with unpredictable activities because their sense of proprioception was still developing. Children lagging in their sense of movement may not understand nonverbal cues they receive from others, such as recognizing that a friend is about to put blocks in their basket.

Infants are born without this sense fully developed. As they grow and move around, their body starts to learn more about itself, like learning a map by heart. At first, infants don't even have an awareness of their own hands, and then one day—ta-dah!—the awareness of hands emerges. The ability to sit still, pay attention, and visually remember the alphabet and numbers depends on children's proprioceptive system.

The proprioceptive system fully develops when children are between eight to twelve years old. This means their brains will have mapped the location of all the muscles, joints, tendons, and ligaments on both sides of their bodies (Bonafede and van der Merwe 2023).

Often children's social and emotional behaviors will parallel the development of their proprioceptive systems. Children who appear to be dysregulated or struggling in these areas need more outdoor free play.

## Educational Implications

Developing proprioceptive systems is the reason young children should sit only for a short time in circle time and should stand in line waiting for as little time as possible. It's not unusual for young children to not yet be able to "feel" their bodies proprioceptively. Some children must constantly move to be able to locate their bodies in space. Other children might wiggle on the floor during circle time or in a chair (maybe even falling out of it) to help better locate their body positions. The year I taught first grade, I had a little girl who could not write comfortably without lying on the floor.

As early childhood educators, we must watch for children who can't proprioceptively locate their thumbs or fingers when trying to hold pencils or crayons as these children are not ready to write. If a child can't locate their fingers, holding pencils or crayons will be difficult because they need more large-motor movement. They'll press too hard or won't be able to control the movement of the crayon. It follows, then, that if their brain has yet to learn to perceive their body in three-dimensional space, writing will be a challenge. This is why introducing writing to children under the age of five is inappropriate. While drawing and mark-making are appropriate and healthy for this age group, expecting a child to produce letters at this stage is both unrealistic and unreasonable given their level of development.

Young children's need for movement cannot be stressed enough. Considering the development of the proprioceptive sense and its impact on learning to read and write, screens and electronics should be limited. These devices are not what young children need for optimal development—and they are not what will support academic growth. Movement is what develops the brain for more structured learning. Carla Hannaford (1995), in her landmark book *Smart Moves*, describes how cognitive development is interwoven with motor development. She asserts that movement helps create and strengthen neural connections in the brain. These connections are essential for learning, memory, and overall cognitive function.

As mentioned above, the act of writing and reading arise inside the proprioceptive sense, as do the creation of sculpture, painting, drawing, writing, building, weaving, sewing, spinning—and the list goes on. It empowers our self-expression!

## Quick Permission Tips:<br>The Proprioception System in Your Setting

Provide opportunities for children to feel tension or pressure in their joints and legs. Things like carrying a heavy stump or stone, hanging from a bar, pushing or pulling something heavy, jumping, and hopping all stimulate and satisfy the need for proprioceptive input.

Reduce the amount of time children use videos, computers, tablets, and other electronics. Children need large amounts of time to play freely inside and outside. A rule of thumb is that children should not sit still for more minutes than twice their age. In other words, a five-year-old needs some large-motor movement after sitting for ten minutes. Children's ability to sit and focus builds slowly.

My Waldorf mentor shared the idea of movement as an in-breath and out-breath. The in-breath is stillness or little movement, and the out-breath is active and has lots of movement. Think of your day as a breathing process:

Arrival to school = Out-breath
Morning Meeting = In-breath
Free play = Out-breath
Storytime = In-breath

Create your day to be a process and flow of in-breaths and out-breaths. If you see fidgeting and difficulty paying attention (in-breath), give the children large-motor movements (out-breath). This is one of the most crucial early childhood classroom management tools.

## Addressing Sensory Issues

The sense of movement is at risk in early childhood. In her groundbreaking book *Smart Moves*, Carla Hannaford points to the importance of large-motor play for cognitive development. Building the body's capacity for movement is a developmental progression that begins with the infant's ability to sit and walk and continues to progress to the ability to write and beyond. Unfortunately, many traditional early childhood teaching settings are not conducive to fostering this movement and even discourage it. We can, however, nurture the sense of movement and support cognitive development with the following:

- Encourage outdoor play that allows children to run, jump, climb, and dig. These activities naturally stimulate the proprioceptive system and help children map their bodies in space.
- Replace sedentary activities with hands-on, movement-based learning experiences. Limit the use of videos, computers, and tablets, as these do not support the development of the proprioceptive sense.
- Create opportunities for children to feel tension or pressure in their joints and muscles. Examples include:
    - Crawling through tunnels or under tables.
    - Rolling large balls or logs.
    - Playing tug-of-war or other resistance-based games.

## THE VESTIBULAR SYSTEM (SENSE OF BALANCE)

Balance only occurs in relationship to something else. It is a perception of position. It allows us to take our place, so to speak, without losing our center. Balance is also referred to as the sense of orientation.

### Balance in Our Language

Our sense of equilibrium infuses everyday speech with metaphors of steadiness and instability, helping us describe things like mental states, emotional control, and reliability: "Has she lost her marbles?," "He'd better steady his emotions," "That man is very stable. I trust him," "They are poised to win," and "That news threw him off balance."

### The Physiology of the Vestibular System

Your sense of balance comes from a special system in your inner ear—think of it like your body's built-in level (like the tool builders use). This system has two main parts:

- Three looped tubes (called semicircular canals) filled with fluid. When you turn your head, the fluid moves around in these tubes, like water in a curved straw when you spin it. This tells your brain which way you're turning.
- Two small pouches (called the utricle and saccule) contain tiny crystals, similar to grains of sand. These crystals rest on top of thousands of tiny hairs. When you tilt your head or move in a straight line, the crystals shift around and bend these hairs, letting your brain know which way is up and how you're moving. All these parts work together to send messages to your brain, helping you stay balanced whether walking, running, or standing still.

### The Role of the Vestibular System in Development

The vestibular system governs our sense of spatial orientation, helping us understand where we are in relation to our environment. It acts as our body's central system for processing sensory information. It integrates all other systems, including vision, and helps us organize everything we do. The vestibular system is the "grand knitter" that creates pathways between systems. When a child spins, they are stimulating the vestibular system. How often have you watched a child turn in circles until they can't stand? They're testing gravity. What may appear to be simple childhood spinning, hopping, swinging, and climbing is actually the hallmark of a fascinating internal process that is paving the way for future growth and development.

## Educational Implications

The vestibular system plays a crucial role in preparing young children for the rigors of elementary school. It is often called the foundation of development. A child's ability to sit upright, track words on a page, and maintain the proper grip of a pencil is a function of a well-developed vestibular system.

Children ages seven years and under need lots of movement to develop a healthy vestibular system. Unfortunately, many early childhood settings are focused on early exposure to worksheets and academic learning that requires a child to sit still and listen. Children need to be able to move freely. Sadly, even recess has been reduced to a minimum in many schools.

## Quick Permission Tips: The Vestibular System in Your Setting

The vestibular needs of young children are often overlooked and yet are foundational to a child's readiness to write and read.

- Floor time for infants is crucial for the healthy development of the vestibular system. Encourage crawling and minimize the use of devices that hold the child and keep them from movement.
- Balance beams are good for practicing linear movements and encouraging vestibular health. Vestibular health is the quality of the link between our inner ear and brain that helps us keep our balance when standing up or navigating uneven surfaces.
- Swinging, slides, stumps of uneven heights to walk across, and play structures to climb are good for vestibular stimulation. Vestibular stimulation is the process through which the vestibular system receives input from a change in head position and thus helps us maintain balance in our bodies.

- Rocking, with the rhythmic, linear movement of back and forth, is the most soothing motion for a child's vestibular system. Consider having a rocking horse in your room.
- Climbing stairs stimulates the linear movement of up and down.
- Bring intentional rotary movement (moving in circles) to your room through circle games and dancing. Go outside and play "Ring Around the Rosies."
- Have some "vestibular fun" by taking the children rolling down a hill!

## Addressing Sensory Issues

Vestibular dysfunction is when a child's brain has trouble understanding how they're moving, how gravity works, or how to keep their balance. As an educator, I observe that many behavioral issues in children can be linked to their sense of balance and how their vestibular system functions. Understanding whether a child feels secure or insecure with movement can help address these behavioral challenges.

There are three main ways these vestibular dysfunctions can show up: hypersensitivity, hyposensitivity, and challenges with bilateral coordination.

### *Extra-Sensitive to Movement (Hypersensitivity)*

These children get motion sick easily in cars, don't like swings or slides, and get dizzy quickly on merry-go-rounds. They might fear falling, get upset when someone tries to move them, and often avoid playground equipment.

Being connected to the earth is a basic need for survival, and the vestibular system plays a key role in how we relate to the ground. We have a natural confidence that we're anchored to the earth, which can be described as gravitational security. Typically, children explore gravity by jumping, swinging, and doing somersaults. However, some children experience gravitational insecurity, which means they feel agitated, fearful, and anxious about falling or the possibility of falling (May-Benson et al. 2020). This fear is basic and instinctual. For these children, movement isn't enjoyable—it feels scary. They often react with a fight, flight, or freeze response:

- Fight response: The child might become angry or resist when someone tries to move them.

- Flight response: The child may avoid activities that involve movement, like riding a bike or swinging because they feel unsafe.
- Freeze response: The child is unable to respond, like standing motionless when asked to take part.

### *Movement Seekers (Hyposensitivity)*

Movement seeking happens when a child's brain can handle a lot of movement and needs a lot of physical activity to stay focused and calm. In this situation, the child looks for ways to challenge gravity and get vestibular stimulation. This might include hanging upside down or bouncing high on trampolines. Such children may become "boosters/crashers," constantly seeking intense movement experiences like jumping from the top of playground equipment or running very quickly.

These children crave linear, straight-line motion, such as rocking back and forth or swinging. They also enjoy rotary motion, spinning around in circles or twirling. Because they always seek new and exciting activities, they rush from one activity to another and may have short attention spans. Their need for continuous movement helps them stay alert and engaged, but it can also make it challenging to focus on tasks that require stillness or low activity.

### *Trouble Using Both Sides (Bilateral Coordination)*

Bilateral coordination is when both sides of your body work together as a team. When your vestibular system is working well, your right and left sides cooperate smoothly. One important skill is called crossing the midline. Imagine an invisible line running down the middle of your body. By age three or four, children should be able to move one hand, foot, or eye across this line into the other side's space. You do this all the time without thinking about it, like when you scratch your opposite elbow, cross your ankles, or read from left to right.

Some children have trouble crossing this midline. When they paint, instead of using one hand to paint across the whole paper, they might switch hands halfway through. These children might also

- have trouble deciding if they're right-handed or left-handed,
- struggle to jump with both feet at once,
- find it hard to catch a ball with both hands, or
- have difficulty using scissors.

Understanding the three major types of vestibular dysfunction—hypersensitivity, hyposensitivity, and challenges with bilateral coordination—can help us recognize issues impacting a child's experience in our classroom. These challenges can affect learning, social interactions, and confidence in physical activities. By identifying and supporting these children's unique needs, caregivers and educators can create an environment that helps them thrive and feel more secure as they grow and learn.

## THE OLFACTORY SYSTEM (SENSE OF SMELL)

Through the olfactory system, we experience the nature and properties of things (bad odors, natural scents, fresh aromas, and so on) and our relationship to them. Our sense of smell is related to memory and can be even more powerful for evoking memories than sight.

### Smell in Our Language

Our olfactory system has deeply permeated everyday speech, giving rise to metaphorical expressions that capture things like intuition, suspicion, and emotional reactions. Think about common phrases we use: "I smell trouble in the air!," "Did you get wind of that?," "She is a breath of fresh air," and "It stinks that we can't have the day off."

### The Physiology of Smell

The organ responsible for the sense of smell is the olfactory mucosa at the root of the nasal cavity. The function of smelling is carried out by two tiny odor-detecting patches comprising almost five or six million yellowish cells that the human nose uses to detect nearly one *trillion* olfactory stimuli.

Smell is the gateway to cellular and body memory. The recognition of smell is immediate, and the sense of smell is connected intimately to the parts of the brain that process emotion and associative learning. Smells can release memories—to identify an odor, we must remember it. When you smell something, your brain quickly recognizes it and connects it with emotions or memories you've stored away. That's why a certain smell can make you feel happy (like when you smell cookies baking) or alert you to danger (like the smell of something burning).

Think of your nose as a radar system that warns about things around you. It lets you know when food has gone bad, alerts you to danger like a broken sewer line, and tells you when something delicious is cooking. When you cry, both your eyes and nose produce tears. Scientists have found that how someone smells can even affect whether we like them (Spence 2021).

## The Role of Smell in Development

We gather messages about our surrounding environment through the sense of smell. We're attuned to our climate with every breath we take by the automatic function of smell that detects dangers, food, and other people. Our sense of smell influences how we recognize each other, how we recall memories, and even how we receive warnings about our environment. For young children, this powerful sensory system helps them build a library of experiences that shapes their understanding of the world, from the comforting scent of a caregiver to the warning smell of smoke. These early olfactory experiences become foundational memories that guide their learning and awareness.

## Educational Implications

The importance of scent communication is often underestimated because it occurs on such an unconscious level. The sense of smell affects the ability to taste and the proper functioning of a human's immune system. Rudolf Steiner (1958) suggested that things around us reveal themselves and their nature through smell.

This sense is a shared reality we can discuss, such as the smell of bread baking or smoke from a fire. It can be a common language through which we can refer to memories and experiences and share an understanding of the associated emotions. For example, many of us associate the feelings of fun and youthfulness with the smell of cut grass on a summer day.

## Quick Permission Tips: The Olfactory System in Your Setting

It is important to recognize that some children may be hypersensitive or hyposensitive to certain smells. Trust a child if they tell you a smell is upsetting to them. Be aware of smell's quality and "truth" in your environment. Artificial smells like those found in many commercial fragrance plug-ins can disturb children's disposition. Some children may be sensitive to these and other synthetic scents.

- Be mindful of the scents of sanitizers, cleaners, and wipes, and choose no scent whenever possible. Synthetic scents can also trigger allergic reactions or asthma in sensitive children.
- Mark the seasons with the smells of nature's gifts: flowers, herbs, and fragrant plants like pine.
- Open the windows and let fresh air circulate when possible.
- Notice how your sense of smell informs you of the health and well-being of the children in your care—it's incredible how much we can smell illness and upset!
- Be mindful of the scents you wear. As a curator of the learning environment, I always took into consideration the experience a child had when giving me a hug. Think about it: they hug us and their faces snuggle right into our bellies. Scents take a direct route to the limbic system and are deeply connected to memory; therefore a comforting smell helps build a positive experience.

I spray my belly with a lovely French perfume by Outremer Eau De Toilette. I have worn it for over thirty years. This scent is so light that I don't smell it after the first few minutes, but everyone else will smell the slightest hint of vanilla that smells like a cake baking. One mom told me that she and her daughter had gone into a local bakery to buy cupcakes and her daughter shouted, "I smell Mrs. Haughey! Do you think she is here?"

## Addressing Sensory Issues

The way children process scents can vary dramatically, making it essential for educators and caregivers to understand and accommodate different sensory needs in the classroom and at home. As we explore sensory processing differences, understanding a child's relationship with smells can help create more supportive learning environments.

Kranowitz (2022) identifies three types of reactions to scents in children:

1. Oversensitive: Some children are highly sensitive to smells, such as those from foods or perfumes, and may respond negatively or with discomfort. For these children, it is important to minimize strong odors. Avoid strong-scented cleaners and classroom products.

2. Craving: Children who crave scents may sniff people, objects, or materials to seek sensory input (even unpleasant smells). Provide these children with appropriate alternatives like scented stickers.
3. Undersensitive: Children who are undersensitive to smells are unaware of odors, including those that indicate danger or hygiene issues (spoiled food, body odor, and similar).

Smell is also firmly bound to body awareness. It can stimulate sympathy or antipathy. This deep connection between scent and our emotional and physical states has led researchers to explore new frontiers in understanding mental health conditions. Researchers are looking into the role of olfactory deficits and dysfunctions in people with depression, migraines, schizophrenia, and even eating disorders (Kohli et al. 2016; Moberg et al. 2014; Sjöstrand et al. 2010).

One final thought about the gift of olfactory awareness: I often am alerted to trouble brewing by my sense of smell in my room. I sometimes wonder, how is it that I "smell" a challenge? Something's in the air that touches my awareness. Teachers and parents don't have eyes in the back of their heads—they have a keen sense of smell!

## THE GUSTATORY SYSTEM (SENSE OF TASTE)

Taste not only shapes children's preferences for what they drink and eat but is also intertwined in their emotional memories. Every time I eat anything with cinnamon, I instantly remember my grandmother's snickerdoodle cookies baking in her home. It brings forth such warm memories.

### Taste in Our Language

We develop a "taste" for what is beautiful and good in life. The sense of taste is deeply connected to our emotions and how we interact with the outside world. Taste occurs on a physical level as we distinguish the characteristics of what we eat (sweet, sour, salty, bitter, and umami) and on an emotional level in defining the experiences: "How sweet!," "That was a bitter pill to swallow," "The memory makes me puke," and "My day was so delicious!"

## The Physiology of Taste

We have approximately two to eight thousand taste buds inside our mouths, including the roofs of our mouths. Each taste bud consists of receptor cells that live for only a few weeks and then are replaced by new receptor cells. While each receptor in a taste bud will respond best to one of the five basic tastes, it can also react to the others.

Below you'll find a brief overview of the five categories of flavor and some of the ways they intersect with one another.

**Bitter**—The bitter flavor performs on a protective level. Its unpleasant taste helps prevent the ingestion of toxic substances.

**Salty**—The salty flavor intensifies the eating experience. Salt suppresses bitterness.

**Sour**—The sour taste buds are another example of protective receptors as they can prevent the ingestion of harmful substances. Sour can be agreeable in small doses.

**Sweetness**—The sweet flavor is an emotionally bonding flavor that stimulates consumption.

**Umami**—The umami flavor tastes savory or meaty. The umami taste receptors in the tongue respond to glutamate and other amino acids in food and send signals to the brain that interpret the flavor as savory.

## The Role of Taste in Development

The gustatory system helps us to nourish and give our bodies health. Our sense of taste goes deep into the very core of our survival, as our taste buds warn us if something isn't consumable. Through the gustatory sense, we differentiate between flavors as we engage with the nourishing aspects of food. As we grow and experience the world around us, we develop a sense of what is edible and what tastes good. The quality of our life will vary according to what kind of food we eat; more proof of how integral our taste buds are for health.

Consider how babies put everything into their mouths—they explore and discover life not only through touch but also through their sense of taste. Perhaps they're developing a "taste" for life!

## Educational Implications

Sharing food is an opportunity to build a sense of community and family as a class. For many children, the educational setting may be the only place they experience sitting at a table participating in a communal meal. These shared mealtimes provide rich opportunities for social learning, language development, and cultural understanding. When early childhood educators create warm, unhurried meal experiences, they help children develop not only healthy eating habits but also crucial social skills like turn-taking, conversation, and respect for others' preferences.

The American College of Pediatricians conducted a review of research on the benefits of the "Family Table" or what they define as shared time together while eating a meal. The benefits are too numerous to state here, but there are a few worth mentioning:

- Shared mealtimes provide children the opportunity to engage in and listen to conversations. This improves language development.
- Time engaged in talking at the table helps children learn important social cues and develop important social skills.

## Quick Permission Tips: The Gustatory System in Your Setting

Many of the children in our care have very limited food choices and likes. It's not unusual for a child to be resistant to trying unfamiliar food. The list below includes some methods for encouraging healthy development around new foods and eating.

- Offer children a tiny portion when introducing new foods.
- Don't force a child to eat what they don't want.
- **Never withhold food from a child for any reason whatsoever.** Food is always an unconditional offering. Our relationship to food touches a very deep place in our sense of trust and security, and we should never use food as a reward or punishment. Recently, a colleague shared how her son had been denied one of the birthday cupcakes at a classroom celebration. The teacher withheld the cupcake because he could not stand still. Her son now cries not to go to school.
- Sharing food is an opportunity to build a sense of community and family as a class. Linger and share stories while eating. Let meals be a time of unrushed joy.

- Talk time is important during meals. Invite conversations at the table.

### Addressing Sensory Issues

Introduce new food flavors and textures to your children gently to encourage healthy gustatory exploration and openness. Never force a child to eat what they reject.

## THE INTEROCEPTION SYSTEM (SENSE OF LIFE/WELL-BEING)

On the most basic level, the interoception sense lets you know if you feel okay. It's that part of you that lets you know if you're tired, thirsty, or hungry. It's also that place inside yourself that can sense time, such as experiencing when it's time for lunch. It's that sense of pain young children experience when they're hungry or thirsty that teaches them what their bodies need. In this way, interoception is deeply rooted in self-awareness and the ability to meet one's needs.

### Interoception in Our Language

Our innate sense of internal vitality and aliveness weaves through our daily expressions, coloring how we describe things like energy, presence, and the essential spark of existence—even in situations where physical life forces aren't literally at play: "She is the life of the party," "He sucked the life out of the room," and "I felt alive again."

### The Physiology of Interoception

People are typically aware of their sense of life when they're not feeling well. It's that inner sense that your well-being is "off," when your internal radar forewarns you that you're getting sick.

The most basic and foundational level of the interoception sense is the sense of life: food, sleep, and nurturance of the physical body. Life itself is held within the rhythms of nature—the rising and setting of the sun, the cycle of the moon, the seasons of a year—upon which we build our personal rhythms. Children require rhythm and they long for it! The more rhythmical a child's life can be, the healthier that child is.

While all aspects of a daily rhythm are important, sleep is a fundamental pillar of a child's routine as it lays the foundation for so many other areas of functioning, like physical growth, neurological development, and circadian rhythms. Sleep profoundly affects how we experience life. It allows us to process the events of the day, creating a foundation of understanding for the past and preparing us for what's to come. In this way, sleep paves the way for and supports the other aspects of interoception, like food and nurturance of the physical body.

## The Role of Interoception in Development

The interoception system is important in a young child's development as it gives them the ability to recognize, interpret, and respond to internal bodily signals. It helps children recognize and respond to cues like hunger, thirst, fatigue, and the need to use the bathroom.

Interoception also helps children develop basic self-care habits, such as brushing teeth, dressing appropriately for the weather, and staying hydrated as they learn to respond to those important internal cues.

## Educational Implications

The assembly line of education can disconnect children from their innate sense of life. This can happen in the following ways:

- Restroom breaks. The typical classroom requires that children ask permission to use the restroom, and they are limited in their ability to do so. This can create anxiety and shame.
- Hunger. Many schools have scheduled lunch or snack times. A child might feel hungry in between these scheduled times, but is often required to "wait until lunch," suppressing their interoceptive awareness.
- Restricted movement. Young children need to move, yet many classrooms require them to sit at circle time and don't allow them to get up.

## Quick Permission Tips: The Interoception System in Your Setting

Here are some of the keys to building a solid and vital sense of life in a child:

- Provide a daily rhythm while the child is developing their sense of life. One of the things I found so powerful in my Waldorf teacher training was that we can influence a child's interoception sense by establishing routines and rhythms. That training asserted that children's sense of life can be measured by their habit body, or their daily rhythms and routines, such as bedtime, waking, eating, and so on. You have likely known a child who has no daily rhythm (and thus no habit body) and have observed the effect that had on their vitality and sense of well-being. If you have a child at home or in class who has great difficulty recognizing their hunger or thirst cues or their need for rest or sleep, a rhythm can be a tremendous therapeutic help.
- Sleeping and waking have a significant impact on the interoception sense. As discussed, sleep routines are fundamental to the rhythm of life. When a child goes to bed at the same general time every night, they begin to feel drowsy as they get ready. How a child is put to bed matters. In my own home, I had nightly little tasks we did as I prepared the children for bed. For example, think of how powerful the gesture of tucking a child into bed can be!
- There is also a rhythm to the digestive system. Giving children meals three times a day at regular times builds a sense of life. If lunch is at a regular time each day, a child's digestive juices will begin to flow as lunchtime approaches! We are not nourished by food alone but also by the rhythm of meals. Researcher José Francisco López-Gil found that having family meals together regularly is significantly associated with better school performance (López et al. 2022). (While our focus here in the PAL model is less on the value of "high achievement scores," we can consider this kind of metric a reflection of children's ability to thrive within the academic environments they find themselves in.) It's not unusual for children with stress-related disorders and problems with social interactions to have meals that are irregular or solitary. Bringing consistency through the classroom's snacks and lunch can help children who might not have this rhythm at home.

- The little routines throughout the day that have their regular place are essential: getting up, washing hands, brushing teeth, brushing hair, sitting down to eat, and so forth. These are small but powerful rhythms. Individuals who do not have this rhythm suffer at some level psychologically—think about people experiencing homelessness as well as others who can take none of these actions for granted. A routine and rhythm bring a deep sense of safety and trust.

### Addressing Sensory Issues

In my experience, many children with ADHD have not fully developed their sense of life. These children cannot step into the rhythm of our days, and it is vital to give them support and understanding. We can support these children by first understanding their experience and their perception of the learning environment, including the tasks they're being asked to complete. As educators, we can aid them by making the necessary adjustments to these, whether through accommodations in the teaching setting such as the seating arrangements and learning materials, the nature of the activities we provide for them, the timing of expectations, or all of these. As a result, children with ADHD will be more equipped to manage the rhythm of their days and will ideally approach this with a sense of openness and confidence versus frustration and overwhelm.

Children with a temperament of anxiety often exhibit this undeveloped sense of life. Observe and see the sense of life in children with behavior issues—what do their daily rhythms look like? How does their sleeping/waking occur? How the family understands the importance of a regular schedule is crucial to their child's ability to experience a sense of life.

## THE AUDITORY SYSTEM (SENSE OF HEARING)

Hearing involves processing various sounds, from the human voice to the sounds of nature to mechanical sounds such as videos, music, and machinery. We hear sounds not only from the external world but also from within.

## Sound in Our Language

Our auditory world has shaped some of the ways we communicate comprehension and connection, giving rise to expressions that turn up in our daily conversations: "I hear you," "Sounds good to me," "That rings true," "That's music to my ears," and "Sound the alarm."

## The Physiology of Sound

When we listen to sounds, we notice three elements: the loudness (volume or strength of the sound), the pitch (whether it's high or low), and the tone (the quality or texture of the sound that sets it apart from others). Sound can also provide us with information that sight cannot. You can see two cups that both look as if they're made of glass, but the sound each makes will tell you if one of those cups is plastic. A person's tone or voice quality can reveal their emotional state when outward appearances don't.

The larynx and vocal folds can resonate in response to many sounds we hear, particularly during speech perception. While high-quality recordings can capture many subtle qualities of sound, there are unique aspects to experiencing live music and voice—including visual, spatial, and social elements—that create a more complete sensory experience. I remember hearing Bach's Concerto for Two Violins in D Minor live for the first time after years of hearing only the recording. I cried because the live performance provided a richer multisensory experience. While modern technology can capture impressive sound quality, children benefit significantly from direct human interaction and live voices during language development.

## The Role of Sound in Development

From the beginning of life, sound plays a vital role in a child's development. The sound of their parent's voice and a favorite lullaby build important connections in attachment and regulation. As children grow, they begin to distinguish between different types of sounds and try to reproduce those sounds—this is the start of communication. Sound is not just about listening but also an active component in the complex process of language acquisition, facilitating both the understanding and the production of speech.

The auditory system gives us the capacity to communicate with others. In this way, it's a social sense, and listening is a social activity. Listening gives us a way to make connection with other human beings. Listening requires us to actively make sense of what we're hearing rather than just passively receiving a sound as an external stimulus. Think of it like this: We hear a friend speaking to us. We've received what they've said, and we consider these words inside of ourselves. It is a meeting of self to sound. *This is listening*. It's within this inner space of processing sound that understanding arises.

## Educational Implications

Being able to listen and process what others are saying is at the core of a child's ability to succeed in a traditional academic setting. Often, however, educators across all grade levels are incredibly fast talkers. Additionally, teachers also tend to speak at one and a half to two grades above the grade level they are teaching. I once read that "89% of the talking that occurs in our classrooms is done by the teacher, not the students" (Hattie 2009). This points to what we looked at in chapter 2 and the assembly line model of education: children treated as empty vessels, not active participants.

## Quick Permission Tips: The Auditory System in Your Classroom

Today's world is full of environmental sounds. Young children are being given headphones for screens and are often flooded with auditory stimuli. Rich experiences of hearing nurture children's ability to process auditory information in an adaptive manner. Here are some strategies to help encourage this process:

- Help young children listen to silence. A moment of silence is so nourishing to the sense of hearing. Invite children to close their eyes and listen to the quiet. Start with just a few seconds, as most children are so dependent on their sight that listening with eyes closed might be a challenge! Build to thirty seconds of silence.
- The quality of your speech and the tone you use can establish a soothing and safe place for children. Even in an environment of mayhem, bring a calm assurance in your voice. It's amazing how your voice alone can settle chaos.

- Sing instructions, commands, and corrections to children in rhymes and fun ditties. I learned this in my Waldorf teacher training. What I witnessed over my twenty-year career is that children processed my singing far better than my speaking.
- Play sound games! Make a sound with an instrument or object inside a box or behind your back and let the children guess what it is. This will build sound discrimination, a crucial skill for language development and literacy.
- If you have a loud class, spend time cultivating the sense of hearing. Remember, it's in listening to one another that the social self finds friendship.
- Play soft and gentle music in your environment as the background.

### Addressing Sensory Issues

One noteworthy issue for young children is an inability to block incoming sound. Visually, we can close our eyes to give ourselves a break. This protective response helps a child self-regulate. Sadly, there is no protective mechanism built into ears. The young child is completely at the mercy of the surrounding sounds, as even placing your hands over your ears often does not block enough incoming sound. We must consider how we're protecting the ears of infants, toddlers, and young children from loud sounds and excessive noise.

Have you ever had a child in your room who could "hear" you but not process your words? I believe this is how children block the overwhelm of sound and incoming stimuli—they shut down internally to protect themselves. They cannot process sound because they have shut down. Unfortunately, this is often perceived by adults as disrespect.

If you have a loud class, spend time cultivating the sense of hearing. I would take moments of stillness when my class was so loud that we could not think or hear one another. Some children have no sense of loudness and need these moments to begin to discriminate.

## THE VISUAL SENSE (SENSE OF SIGHT)

Ninety percent of the information we take in about our environment is through the eyes. In her book *The Out-of-Sync Child*, Carol Kranowitz (2022, 183) reveals that "eyesight is not the same as vision. . . . Eyesight is a prerequisite for vision. Vision, unlike sight, is not a skill we are born with but rather one we develop gradually as we integrate our senses."

## Sight in Our Language

Visual perception illuminates our metaphors, giving us powerful ways to describe emotional impact, personal presence, uncertainty, and obvious needs: "His attitude dimmed the room," "Did you see how she glowed?," "The lines are blurred on that topic," and "His need for a rest is glaring."

## The Physiology of Sight

Our sense of vision is one of the most critical ways we gather information about the world around us. It allows us to detect light, recognize colors, and identify shapes, patterns, and objects. The human eye is highly specialized and works like a camera, capturing light and sending the information to the brain for processing. This is how we understand what we see.

Our eyes aren't just focused on what's directly in front of us—they can also sense motion and detect objects in our peripheral vision. This ability helps us react quickly to changes in our environment, like noticing a ball rolling toward us or spotting something moving in the corner of our vision.

Rudolf Steiner, a philosopher and scientist, proposed an interesting idea about how our eyes work. He suggested that our eyes act like extra limbs, constantly "reaching out" into the world to gather information and bring it back to us (Steiner 1958). While this isn't a literal description, it highlights how active and dynamic the process of seeing is—our eyes are always scanning, focusing, and adapting to help us make sense of everything we encounter visually.

## The Role of Sight in Development

Sight plays a role in how you understand and interact with the world around you. This visual information helps your brain make sense of people and your environment in amazing ways. When you look at someone's face, your visual system picks up subtle facial expressions that indicate if they're happy, sad, angry, or confused. Your eyes also notice body language, like when someone crosses their arms or stands confidently, and gestures like pointing or waving. Your brain processes all these visual signals to help you understand what others are feeling and thinking.

Your visual system also helps you learn how the physical world works. As light enters your eyes and reaches your retina, your brain creates detailed mental maps of your surroundings. Through vision, you observe cause-and-effect relationships, like how a ball follows a curved path when thrown or how ripples spread across water when something splashes into it. Your visual cortex processes information about movement, depth, and spatial relationships, helping you understand gravity, motion, and how objects interact.

## Educational Implications

There is a misconception that the more instructional materials we have on our walls, the more children are learning, when in fact the opposite is the truth. Young children are growing and developing their sensory integration. Visual noise is both visually and emotionally distracting and difficult for them to process. The only way a child has to block the visual noise around them is to close their eyes, disengage, and perhaps even emotionally withdraw from their surroundings.

It's not uncommon for the walls and shelves of the early childhood setting to be filled with visual noise:

- Bright, primary colors filling the environment through toys, manipulatives, and materials that clutter the space
- Loud posters and decorated bulletin boards in themes and cutouts (shapes, numbers, letters, animals, and more!) cluttering the walls
- Bright, themed rugs for circle time creating a distraction

## Quick Permission Tips: The Visual System in Your Setting

Reducing visual noise is critical for creating an optimal play-activated learning environment. Consider the following to help you create a warm, soothing setting conducive to exploration and learning:

- Use calm, warm colors in the environment. I like to use brown, neutrals, and greens as the three main colors that unify my room.

- Don't over-label your environment. If you're required to label, choose what has the most meaning to the children. Unless referenced and used intentionally, most labeling becomes visual noise.
- Leave blank spaces on your walls for children to have visual rest. This is crucial for children who have difficulty with visual processing.
- Place plants on shelving and in windows. Gazing at nature is calming to the nervous system.
- Strive for a home-like environment, not a school-like environment.

### Addressing Sensory Issues

In a study by Stephanie Bolin (2015), when the visual noise was increased in the preschool classroom, there was a dramatic increase in "violence, disobedience, lack of compliance, overexcitement, refusal to participate/interact with others, irritability, difficulty focusing, decrease of ability to concentrate, and an increase in fidgeting and restless behavior" (2). That's a list of potential outcomes that can't be ignored in the early childhood setting. Avoid adding to these issues by having a visually calm environment.

## PERMISSION AND THE SENSES

We've covered extensive ground in this chapter and have examined the role of the sensory system and eight ways in which it is expressed. (See Review of the Senses in the Environment in appendix B, pages 153–154 for a form to help you review the eight sensory systems.)

With this, we now have a framework of understanding that it is not anecdotal—it is based in science and physiology. It is a view of our wonderfully complex human design that will inform and support the application of the next three phases of the PAL model in the following chapters.

When we can fully understand the role of the sensory system in children's development, we can fully embrace the "why" of what we're doing as educators. While we can acknowledge the validity and honor of our instincts when it comes to teaching children in the healthiest and most developmentally appropriate ways, with this basis of knowledge we can stand firm in the truth of what is effective and *right*. Armed with this information, we're also equipped to educate and inform those who may question or lack understanding of play-based learning and its efficacy. Put simply, we can say with confidence—it's not just a "nice idea," it's science.

The early childhood classroom should be a space built with permission—permission to move, get messy, and explore. One of our top priorities is giving children the freedom to express themselves through exploration and experimentation using all their senses. When young children have permission to follow their sensory needs, they play in the areas of the environment that meet their needs.

## GOLD NUGGETS

- The sensory system is the doorway to learning for young children. Children receive information about the world around them through the sensory receptors that then transmit the incoming input to the brain.
- Our environments provide a palette of sensory experiences. In many ways, this is the tangible curriculum for the child.
- The early childhood classroom should be a space built with permission—permission to move, get messy, and explore.

## THE PRACTICE OF THE EDUCATOR: PREPARING

Take an inventory of your classroom and learning spaces with children's sensory needs in mind. Below I have collected some of my favorite ways of looking at my space and actions in light of the sensory systems.

### *Visual Sense*

- How can my classroom environment visually communicate safety? Are pathways clear, and is there adequate lighting?
- How can I use visual elements (colors, natural light, artwork) to provide a sense of calm and belonging?

- Do my visual aids or classroom decorations reflect diversity, encouraging inclusivity and connection among children?
- How can I use visuals to reflect children's identities, interests, and accomplishments, nurturing a sense of pride and belonging?

> *Aha Note!*
> Our task is to prepare an environment that gives permission to children's sensory growth and development.

### *Auditory Sense*

- Is the noise level in my classroom managed to prevent sensory overload? Are there quiet zones?
- Do I have noise-canceling tools for students who need auditory breaks?
- How can I be more mindful of children's hearing sensitivities?
- How can I use sound (e.g., songs, storytelling, rhythm games) to build community and connection?
- Am I mindful of my own voice and tone? Am I using my voice as a tool of connection and not of compliance?

### *Tactile Sense*

- Where do I provide children the freedom to touch, press, squeeze, and explore textures without hearing "no"?
- Have I provided soft, varied, and accessible textures that allow children to self-soothe or engage in sensory play?
- Do I bring activities that involve touch in a way that nurtures trust and bonding (group projects, tactile games)?

### *Olfactory Sense*

- Am I keeping the environment free from strong or overwhelming odors that may be distressing for children?
- Are there natural or familiar scents (e.g., plants, baking smells) that could enhance children's sense of comfort and belonging?

- What sensory experiences could I bring around smell that could encourage curiosity or cultural connection (e.g., smelling spices or flowers)?

### *Gustatory Sense*

- Are there opportunities in my classroom for children to explore tastes in a noncoercive, open environment where they feel free to say yes or no to trying new foods?
- Do I give children permission to express their taste preferences without judgment?
- Have I included taste activities designed to include diverse cultural foods and preferences?
- Can children in my class make choices about their participation in taste experiences, enhancing their sense of control?

### *Proprioceptive Sense*

- How does my classroom layout encourage safe and independent movement, giving children permission to explore their space freely?
- What activities or tools (e.g., yoga, weighted items, resistance bands) can I use to help children meet their proprioceptive needs?
- Am I bringing physical activities and games that build teamwork and cooperation?

### *Vestibular Sense*

- How does my environment support children in exploring movement in ways that feel safe and fun, promoting a sense of "Yes, I can do this"?
- Are there safe spaces in my class for children to swing, spin, or climb, enhancing their confidence in spatial awareness?
- Am I providing safe, developmentally appropriate tools (e.g., wobble stools, balance beams, rocking chairs) that support vestibular engagement?

### *Interoceptive System*

- Does my environment encourage children to listen to their own bodies, giving them the autonomy to say yes to their needs for hydration, hunger, or rest?
- Do I model and encourage permission for students to listen to their bodies without fear of judgment (e.g., asking for water or a break)?
- What tools or strategies (e.g., breathing exercises, sensory breaks) can I provide to support students in regulating their internal states?
- How do I create a culture where students feel safe expressing their emotions and physical needs?

CHAPTER 4

# Choice

The self is not something ready-made, but something in continuous formation through choice of action.
—John Dewey

## Choice Pillar

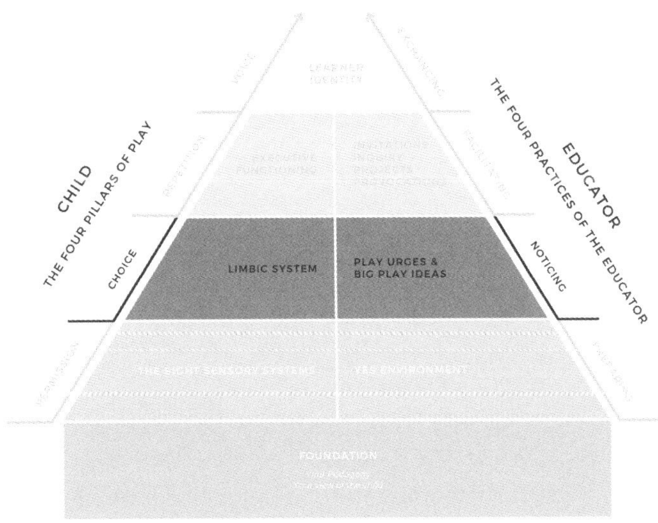


"Look! Look!" Claire, a joyful child with wild and curly blond hair, is screaming.

It's recess and the children are gathering around Claire on the playground. I make my way over only to discover a little family of turtles.

"Can we give them a home?" Claire begs.

"Why not?" I think to myself. I go and grab a box to bring the turtles to the classroom with us, and we spend the morning preparing a home for them in a big aquarium. We gently put the turtle family in their new digs and delight in watching them explore their surroundings. The children talk about what their names are and who is the daddy and mommy. Baby is clear—she's the little one.

The next day we arrive back at the classroom only to discover a startling but honest fact. Turtles poop. And there is now lots of poop. All over the new habitat. I shake my head and tell the children this is not the best place for the turtles. There is nowhere for them to poop, and I don't want to clean up after them every day. (Cleaning up turtle poop is not my idea of play!)

We pack up the turtles, take them back outside, and release them into the woods by the school, away from the playground. As we walk back into the classroom, several students are sad and crying. My heart is hurting for them. It's challenging to navigate the waters of loss for most children, and this was no exception.

"Can we write them?" Claire cries. "I don't want the baby turtle to think I'm mad at her." Soon the children are crowding around the writing center and constructing letters to the turtles. And as luck would have it, the turtles write back.

A long and beautiful relationship began with the turtle family, and a powerful, natural impulse to write and communicate on paper was born. It was one of the most memorable studies in my teaching career, fueled by Claire's passion for caring for the turtles and her ability to be heard and have a choice about following that passion.

The second pillar of the Play-Activated Learning (PAL) model is Choice. This is where we harness the power of play to engage children and their interests, and it all begins with the power to choose. According to the Merriam-Webster dictionary, choice is an act of selecting or making a decision when faced with two or more possibilities.

Choice is all about experimenting and discovering. It's a joyful stage of play, and it's also a crucial one that we don't want to push children past too quickly. Let them dwell in that exploration because this is all about the limbic system, as this stage of positive emotional engagement activates the brain's reward system. It triggers the chemical dopamine, that feel-good reward chemical that tells us, "Yes." The pleasure of play is literally priming the brain for further learning. This is why this phase is so crucial.

In this chapter, we'll consider the powerful role choice plays in the unfolding of the child's self and learning and, ultimately, their unique brilliance. We'll also look at using informed observation to nurture the groundwork for the phases that follow (repetition, voice, and children's identities as learners). Through our educators' practice of noticing in this stage, we'll be able to facilitate play urges and big play ideas conducive to and nurturing of children's sense of choice.

## THE FOUR DIMENSIONS OF CHOICE

To provide context and a deeper understanding of the role of choice in children's learning and development, let's investigate how the expectations of traditional education hinder play. To illustrate this clearly, let's look at the four dimensions of choice in play.

A core tenet of the PAL model is respecting children's right to choose during play. As their teacher and guide, I create an environment that empowers children to make choices that align with their interests, needs, and development.

### *The Four Dimensions of Choice*

| DIMENSION OF CHOICE | RIGHT | TRADITIONAL SETTING | IMPACT |
|---|---|---|---|
| **Where to Play** | RIGHT to choose where to play | Teachers predetermine the number of children in each area. | Limits children's agency and intrinsic motivation. |
| **Who to Play With** | RIGHT to choose who to play with | Teachers assign play partners and areas. | Restricts social interactions and cooperative skills development. |
| **What to Play With** | RIGHT to choose what to play with | Predetermined activities with right and wrong ways to execute. | Hinders creativity and intrinsic motivation. |
| **How to Play** | RIGHT to choose how to play | Materials and activities have intended uses and learning goals. | Limits original ideas and innovative thinking. |

And one more right: the right to decline participation. While children sometimes need gentle encouragement to take part in activities, "forcing" them to do so—particularly with punitive undertones—undermines the inherent value of participation and creates an adversarial dynamic that can taint the entire learning experience. While this right isn't included in the above table, it will be given further context later in this chapter.

## RIGHT TO CHOOSE WHERE TO PLAY

This is the beginning of play—choosing where to do so. With this right, the child can genuinely play versus having to adapt their natural drives to fit within the confines they're given. Giving children the freedom to choose where they want to play is trusting that their choice is driving their growth and development. Just as we trust that a ten-month-old's choice to pull up on a coffee table drives the development of their legs and core muscle strength that are crucial for walking, we can trust that play is driving cognitive growth for the four-year-old in the block center.

### Obstacles to Choice in Traditional Settings

To manage the noise level and compliance of the room, most traditional settings establish the number of children who can play in each area or center. No more than the established limit of children can enter the space. Let's explore three common population control practices teachers use in the classroom and their potential drawbacks:

- Assigned centers—Preselecting which centers or activities each child can access prevents self-directed exploration. Being confined to a teacher-chosen area inhibits agency and intrinsic motivation.
- Rotating centers—Having children rotate through stations on a fixed schedule restricts sustained engagement in self-selected play. Regular transitions break focus and disrupt social connections, making it hard for children to develop sustained focus and attention.
- Limited center population—Capping the number of children allowed in each learning area removes the child's ability to choose where to play. It can create stress and upset as some children may not have an opportunity to

play where they wish and may feel excluded from their chosen groups and desired activities.

### Strategies for Overcoming Challenges

Some of you may be wondering, "What do I do if all the children choose to play in blocks or home living? How do I manage it? What if fights break out because there are not enough materials for everyone?" Two strategies have worked for me for over twenty-five years.

#### *Expand the Desired Area*

If there is high demand for a certain area of the environment, I adapt it and expand the space to accommodate the number of children who want to play there. For example, I had a setting of four-year-olds who loved building bridges with blocks. Ten children would rush to play there, so I expanded the center to accommodate ten children. What came from that adaptation was some extraordinary play around the story of "The Three Billy Goats Gruff," and it included an autistic child who engaged in parallel play for the first time in our setting. I have found over and over that expanding the space to accommodate the children makes way for miracles to happen.

#### *Discuss Possibilities*

Sometimes there are not enough materials in an area, so children argue and fight. First, I give the children time to work it out. Most often they will figure out a solution if we give them time and space. Other times, the lack of materials may cause ongoing problems. In these situations, I like to sit down in that area and talk to the children who are struggling. There are not enough materials. What can we do? What might work? I write down all of the ideas and thoughts they share, and we work together to find a solution that the children will then test. It's a wonderful opportunity to build problem-solving skills.

## RIGHT TO CHOOSE WHO TO PLAY WITH

Choosing who to play with is an essential right in the classroom. It is the foundation of building the social self. The right to choose who to play with allows children to navigate social interactions and build cooperative skills.

Giving children the freedom to choose play partners builds essential skills of socially competent behavior. Allowing organic peer interactions guided by children's instincts promotes growth across social, emotional, cognitive, and communication domains in developmentally appropriate ways.

## Obstacles to Choice in Traditional Settings

Many settings assign children to play in specific areas for a specific amount of time with other prechosen children. In this scenario, children are not allowed to pick who they play with. Let's take a look at how assigned and rotating centers can also predetermine who gets to play with who:

- Assigned centers—Preselecting where the children play removes not only the child's right to choose where to play but also the ability to pick who to play with. This stifles social development.
- Rotating centers—Having children rotate through stations allows educators to pick who is in each rotating group. This makes it more difficult for children to develop friendships.

## Strategies for Overcoming Challenges

You might be wondering, what if a child struggles with choosing or making friends? I consider this an important opportunity to support the child in nurturing their social relationships. I will observe and then ask myself what their interests are and what they would enjoy playing.

One of the best techniques I have used is to shadow these children, as they often need help in their interactions. I will use the "newscaster" strategy, announcing what the other children are doing like I'm broadcasting the news. For example, when I taught three-year-olds, I had one child whom the other children did not like playing with because he grabbed toys. I began shadowing him and broadcasting what was happening. "Sarah is building a tower and Gary is helping her stack the blocks." "Gary's arm knocked over the top of the tower. Sarah is helping to put the blocks up."

The key to newscasting is to state just the facts. Leave out any subjective statements. In doing so, you are helping the child become aware of the other children's play. In my experience, children who struggle with play relationships struggle with reading the environment. It's amazing how quickly this technique can help nurture a child's capacity to play with others.

## RIGHT TO CHOOSE WHAT TO PLAY WITH

Exercising the right to choose what to play with allows children to explore materials that match their innate curiosity and interests. By rotating a thoughtfully curated selection of open-ended materials, we allow children to fluidly choose items that provide the right novelty, challenge, and interest level to stretch their development meaningfully. Trust their instincts!

### Obstacles to Choice in Traditional Settings

The traditional early childhood teacher designs the day and its activities according to a theme or topic. These theme-based activities are often placed in centers or learning stations.

Let's look at those activities. More often than not, the activities are closed-ended, and there is a "right or wrong" way to do them. An example is a sink-and-float science activity or tracing a letter on a worksheet.

There is no choice in the way the activity is done, and the thinking has been done for the child. The educator has decided how the children are to execute the activity, usually to show a specific learning outcome. Again, this offers children a rigid container in which to explore and learn within the context of the "right or wrong" nature of these activities.

This approach dampens the natural tendency in young children to experiment, explore, and play with their own ideas. Children can become hesitant to take risks because they may get it "wrong."

Perhaps the most worrisome impact is that it drives external motivation to "get it right" and be rewarded for that achievement. This not only undermines children's natural curiosity but can create unnecessary anxiety. In kindergarten, my daughter Liz would come home and pretend "practice" the worksheets she was given in school. I mistakenly assumed she was just playing school. One day I sat down and asked her if I could join her school play. "No Mommy," she said with tears, "I must practice so I don't make any more mistakes. Mrs. Bailey tells everyone when I do it wrong." My heart fell. I had no idea she was feeling so much pressure. At the same time, I was amazed at how she had taken up playing as a way to work out her anxiety.

### Strategies for Overcoming Challenges

The most powerful strategy any educator can take, regardless of context and setting, is to shift the focus from achieving a specific outcome to valuing the process of learning. Recognize children's efforts rather than focusing on whether they got it "right" or "wrong." Encourage risk-taking without fear of failure.

Young children deserve to be free of pressure to perform. Yet, globally, this is the reality. We can do better. Academic-driven outcomes have no place in early childhood.

## RIGHT TO CHOOSE HOW TO PLAY

When children are free to use materials in any way they desire, without adult-imposed limitations, it sparks original ideas and innovative thinking. When play is teacher-driven, children become reliant on extrinsic motivation. Giving children the freedom to choose how they play piques their intrinsic drive to learn through play they find meaningful.

### Obstacles to Choice in Traditional Settings

It has been a practice for decades in traditional early childhood settings to confine materials to designated areas. It was often looked upon as teaching children the order of things. The predetermined activities and materials are expected to be used in the intended way to fulfill the learning goal or outcome.

What I find interesting is that cross-pollination doesn't eliminate order. Cross-pollination is allowing materials to intermingle across different learning areas within the environment. Rather than confining specific items to isolated areas, cross-pollination allows materials to move across the room. In fact, order and everything having a "home" is essential to the success of this process.

Cross-pollination is a natural outcome of open-ended play as children make connections across materials. Blending items sparks experimentation and builds cognitive flexibility. Restricting the movement of materials is restricting the growth and development available to the children.

In one example of creativity that I love, a child took the LED tea lights from blocks into home living to make the burners "light up." She turned on the tea lights and pretended to cook dinner for her family.

### Strategies for Overcoming Challenges

Cross-pollination does not mean allowing a complete free-for-all. At the beginning of the year, I let the children know what must not leave its area. The only things I restrict are things like paint and glue that can damage materials in other areas. I normally put the art area off limits for cross-pollination except for a special shelf with paper, markers, and tape. Sometimes I will put playdough off limits, depending on the flooring in my environment. If the idea of cross-pollination scares you, start with just two areas of the environment where you will allow it, such as blocks and home living.

In my experience, cross-pollination is difficult if you have not established homes for everything in your environment. Order is essential for the effective use of cross-pollination in the teaching setting. I promise you this, cross-pollination will become a required part of your setting once you experience its magic.

## THE ROLE OF ORDER IN YOUR SETTING

I want to talk for a moment about order in the environment of choice. When I refer to order, I am talking about materials having a designated home. This is crucial for the maintenance of the environment. If you do not teach the children where everything belongs, you'll end up doing most of the care and cleaning up of your classroom yourself.

### Everything Has a Home

Having a home for everything lays the foundation for cleanup, and it is fundamental. We must establish the location of each item in each center.

- This process will take time.
- This is one reason for limiting the quantity of the materials.
- It is time-consuming until the children learn where each home is.

Visually labeling a material's designated home is a huge help for children when they are finding where to return materials at cleanup time and self-checking that they've done it correctly. I start the year with limited materials so the children have more ease at pickup time. Once the children have mastered putting things back where they belong, I add more materials. Establishing cleanup as a set routine will pay off immensely as the materials expand in the setting's environment.

One final tip about cleanup: your mindset about cleanup is everything. Think of it not as the end of playtime but as a separate and important part of your day. Be sure to provide enough time for the children to fully pick up. At the beginning of the year, I allow at least twenty minutes at the end of the day for cleaning up the classroom environment.

## Sing and Play as We Clean

Children respond to songs and games more than commands. Here are some of my favorite cleanup songs.

### *Everyone Pick Up!*

(To the tune of "London Bridge Is Falling Down")

Everyone pick up, pick up, pick up. Everyone pick up in our classroom.

All of the [buttons] here, [buttons] here, [buttons] here. All of the [buttons] here, in our classroom.

Put the [logs] on the shelf, on the shelf, on the shelf. Put the [logs] on the shelf, in our classroom.

### *This Is the Way We. . .*

(To the tune of "This Is the Way")

This is the way we pick up blocks, pick up blocks, pick up blocks.

This is the way we pick up blocks

As we clean up.

### *I See Something*

(To the tune of "Are You Sleeping Brother John")
I see something, I see something

Out of place, out of place

It does not belong there

It does not belong there

Please show me where, show me where

Here are some favorite games we play.

### *Go, Go, Stop!*

In this simple but effective game, everyone picks up when you say "Go." When you say "Stop," everyone freezes. It is a little like red light/green light and is also excellent for building executive function. "Go, go, go, go, STOP!"

### *What Do You Notice?*

Gather in a circle before whole-group time. Have the children glance around the room and identify what center is the messiest. Ask for volunteers to clean that area for the class.

## RIGHT TO DECLINE PARTICIPATION

When we respect children's right to decline participation, it helps them develop self-awareness and listen to their internal cues. Additionally, it models consent and sets healthy boundaries. This empowers self-advocacy.

The idea that children must do as they are told is so deeply ingrained in our culture that we can't even see it. As we looked at in chapter 2, compliance has been the underlying goal of the assembly line model of education, and to dare suggest children can decline participation is outrageous. If we don't force a child to participate in "circle time," they are pushing the boundaries of the classroom.

There is another way of looking at this that preserves classroom boundaries and honors the child's choice. The right to decline is reliant on a mutual respect between the child and educator. One year Abby, an active four-year-old, declined to come to our morning meeting at first. She would sit in the library center and read books. Abby's absence did not provoke the other children to join her because morning meetings were a very important time in the classroom. There was high energy as the children shared their perspectives and cocreated the day with me. Six weeks into our school year, Abby came to our meeting and joined the planning. The entire class erupted in clapping and cheers. Her participation mattered to her peers, and my coteacher and I were in tears watching how much the children cared for each other. This is what arises when we honor children's choices.

## CHOICE AND THE RIGHTS OF CHILDREN

The heart of child-led learning is giving children free choice when playing. It's not unusual to see educators utilizing population control strategies during playtime even in "play-based" settings. When we control children's right to choose where to play, we remove choice and interest. When we restrict choice in play, we restrict growth and development.

To further illustrate the role of choice in children's academic development, it's helpful to compare learning models that are teacher-directed versus play-activated, as outlined in the table below:

### *Learning Models Compared*

| TEACHER-DIRECTED LEARNING<br>Typically Theme Based | PLAY-ACTIVATED LEARNING<br>Interest-Based |
|---|---|
| • Curriculum and activities are planned by the teacher.<br>• The teacher focuses on academic skills or growth and developmental benchmarks.<br>• The teacher selects themes and materials and directs the learning process.<br>• Assessment focuses on standardized testing and benchmarks.<br>• The teacher talks/lectures more and children listen.<br>• There is "one-size-fits-all" instruction.<br>• Children are viewed as "empty vessels" to be filled with meaningful learning. | • Play-activated learning emerges from children's interests and curiosity. It is grounded in the young child's innate drive to play.<br>• Play-activated learning is driven by children's interests.<br>• Children make choices and lead their play.<br>• Assessment happens through observation, individual portfolios, and reflection.<br>• Intrinsic motivation is prioritized through choice.<br>• Children are seen as capable, competent learners filled with potential.<br>• Play is understood as learning. |

The Reggio Emilia approach greatly influenced my view of the child. In the mindset of the Western tradition of the past several centuries, and within the context of the assembly line paradigm, children are not considered old enough yet to be citizens, and schools are institutions where children learn to comply by obeying the rules set by the education system. The Reggio Emilia approach opened a revolutionary perspective by viewing the child as a citizen with inherent rights and competencies. This idea has inspired me profoundly in my own practice. How could I make my room a place where the children in my care are citizens who are bearers of rights? And what would their rights be?

When we begin to break down the average day most young children experience in a child care center or preschool, we see they're offered very little choice, if any. What are the ramifications of this "no choice" curriculum design? In the next section, we'll explore what children miss out on by following a curriculum with little or no choice. To truly understand the enormous benefits of making choices and allowing self-selection for young children, we turn to brain science.

## EXECUTIVE FUNCTION

To truly understand the enormous benefits of allowing choices and self-selection for young children, we turn to brain science. When children make decisions and push away distractions, they build their executive functioning, their ability to focus, plan, and attend to tasks. These interconnected skills allow us to carry out critical everyday tasks. Choice in play helps children block out distractions, builds focus and sustained attention, and develops a deep level of engagement. Let's look at each one.

### Increases Ability to Block Out Distractions

The ability to tune out distractions is based in executive function. When we give children a choice in play, they are engaging in the task of competing interests. They have to choose: where am I going to play? It sounds simple, but it's a significant challenge for a young child who is just beginning to develop executive function.

The magic ingredient is interest. An interest can be a magnet for a young child's attention, helping them block distractions. When a child repeatedly practices blocking distractions, the neural pathways of sustained attention are being developed.

## Builds Focus and Sustained Attention

Consider this: Children are not born with executive function, yet in play, they can sustain their focus for long periods. When children choose their play, they are more likely to become highly focused because it's important to them.

Let's imagine the traditional classroom oriented around centers, but, in this program, the children choose where they want to play and how long they'll stay.

First, they must choose between different learning centers. This first step can be overwhelming! "Do I want to play with the goopy goo? Or sort color items?" As adults, we're making decisions all day long, often without even being conscious of them, and it's no big deal. However, to a young child, this is a new and developing skill and can be challenging. Being allowed time and space to make choices is an important facet of their play-based education.

Next, once children choose where to spend their time, they then choose how long they'll play there. Some of you must be wondering, "Sally! Don't they need to learn to stay and not keep moving from center to center?" My question for you is, how is that going for you and the children in your care? Really. What's the impact of requiring young children to stay and play in a space where they don't want to be? It's not unusual for young children to wander from place to place as they develop the capacity to focus and sustain their attention.

You may notice that children become easily engrossed in screen time for long amounts of time and ask whether this means they are learning to focus. Watching a program or show on TV, however, does not develop sustained attention. Instead, too much screen time can cause damage. Researchers Angeline Lillard and Jennifer Peterson (2011) examined the immediate impact of different types of television on young children's executive function. The study showed that children who watched a fast-paced television cartoon performed significantly worse on executive function tasks than children who watched educational television or drew a picture. The study concluded that fast-paced television viewing can immediately negatively impact executive function in young children. The rapid changes in image and scene in entertainment television programs hold a child's attention. However, it affects an entirely different system of the brain than the regions associated with healthy, sustained focus.

### Develops a Deep Level of Engagement

Over time, children will discover the activities that satisfy their play urges (schemas) at a deep level. When they're in a play space that is attending to their developmental needs, they stay. Children have a natural focus and attention driven by curiosity and interest. At this point in their lives, the brain is building the neural pathways of attention. This is not being developed when we set timers and require children to stay in a center where they have no interest.

## THE LIMBIC SYSTEM

Imagine you could turn on a light switch for learning in a child's brain so they would be ready and eager to learn. This switch exists, and I will show you how to flip it on. By now, we hopefully can agree that children's interest in play prepares their brains for learning. Each child's full choice and interest in play affects their brain, including its readiness and ability to learn and to remember that learning.

When you're interested in something and it feels like precisely what you were looking for, how is your attention span? Pretty darn good, right? This joy and pleasure are critical for developing executive function. Play has had a bad rap for decades because it is fun—but the *fun* part of play is what unleashes the power of executive function.

When children choose where, what, and who they play with, chances are good that they will become deeply engaged. Research like that of Kate Witt, David Harper, and Bart Ellenbroek (2024) has examined the role of dopamine in play. Here's my take on it. Self-chosen play activates the limbic system, which is like a light switch. The limbic system is a group of brain structures that regulates our emotional and behavioral responses, as well as motivation and memory. When pleasure and joy are involved, the limbic system is turned on. This releases dopamine, which is the "Yes, I want more" chemical. The limbic system (our "primal" brain) is like a radar system. It will assess what is happening and search for connections to help us feel safe and secure. When connection is established, the limbic system can relax and allow the brain to function fully. The limbic system is also the seat of emotions. When the limbic system interprets incoming sensory information, it is determining the emotional value of the information. The interpretation of sensory information is based on the child's prior experiences and the current event combined. Both what has happened to the child and what is currently happening give context to how the child will experience the information: what thoughts will be associated with it, such as "this feels good" or "this feels scary," and how they will respond to the information.

Imagine the following scenario:

> A four-year-old child enters the setting and sees new materials in the block center. This sensory information is interpreted as exciting, and the child is motivated to go to the block center to play. The child begins to think about playing with the new materials and what activities they will be doing in the block center.

This positive sensory information sends a message of interest and excitement and directs behavior toward a purpose. It motivates children to be in action and enhances their capacity to think and learn.

Now imagine this scenario:

> A four-year-old child enters the setting and sees worksheets set out and the teacher asking everyone to be quiet and sit down to do the work. This sensory information is interpreted as a negative, and the child is angry. The educator does not consider the child's inner need to move and play to be appropriate in this scenario.

This negative sensory information turns the "light switch" for learning off, which means thinking and motivation are turned off (or at least significantly turned down). Whether the child "should" be interested in an activity is of no importance.

Emotions, regulated by the limbic system, can either support or disrupt learning. How children perceive a situation is what brings about their emotional response, which triggers specific neurotransmitters that then affect their potential for learning in that moment. Since young children are wired emotionally for play, environments that discourage self-initiated play naturally disrupt the desire to learn (Tyng et al. 2017).

> Imagine a child is playing deeply in the dramatic play center. Rich conversations and pretend play are happening. Then, the teacher rings a little bell. "Time to move to your next center."

> Imagine another scenario in which a child goes to play in the dramatic play center to pick up where she and her friends left off the day before.

> The teacher comes over and says, "This center is full. Pick somewhere else to play. Only five children are allowed to be here."

In both cases, there is a disruption in the children's positive emotional connections with the setting. Scenarios such as these can turn off the switch. Some children are able to bounce back and move on with apparent ease, but others are left upset and with a need for play that cannot be met.

Even for the child who bounces back, the desire and capacity for learning has been dampened by the emotional response, however slight, that comes from having to drop an exciting activity and move on to something else. The light may not have been completely switched off, but it has been dimmed.

Children's biochemistry and moods are regulated by connections formed within the relationships in the setting. The limbic system is also like a Wi-Fi hub that transmits and receives signals to and from other people. Children need connections with their classmates more than anything else in the early childhood environment. Neuroscientist Jaak Panksepp (1998) said play is the drive for social bonding. The relationship between social connection and learning works like this:

- Children need play for social connection.
- Social connection stimulates motivation.
- Motivation drives interest.
- Interest builds the executive functioning of the brain.
- Executive functioning sets the child up for success in academic learning.

Let's peek at the brain chemical responsible for motivation, to understand its role within the limbic system and how it activates the desire to learn. The chemical dopamine is a messenger between brain cells. The brain releases it when children eat their favorite food or play in their favorite center, bringing feelings of satisfaction as part of the reward system. "Do this again!" is the basic message of dopamine.

When children return to the block center every day to build with their friends and pretend they're superheroes, their dopamine levels continuously signal how enjoyable or worthwhile the situation is in a reward feedback loop. The rewards, in this case, could be the social bonding and the satisfaction of the play environment.

Here's where things get really interesting: dopamine can also be thought of as the "save button" in the brain. When dopamine is present during an event such as the block play we just talked about, children are more likely to remember that event

(Burns 2012). When dopamine is absent, children are less inclined to remember it. In other words, when dopamine is present in the learning environment, the learning sticks. This is obviously a strong case for a learning environment that stimulates motivation and reward in a child's brain! The wonderful and fascinating pathway leading from a child's interests to the ideal outcome of a strong foundation for learning generally unfolds this way:

- A child's personally driven interests and wants in play begin an orchestra of amazingness that leads to motivation and learning.
- Self-initiated play (which is intrinsically motivating), built from interest and curiosity, engages the limbic system, turning it on.
- The positive emotions created in the limbic system drive a child to instinctively want to engage in an activity.
- The brain's reward system releases dopamine and brings a deep satisfaction in the social connections and learning taking place.
- The dopamine release sets up a chemical reward loop that drives a child to return to this play that brought such satisfaction.

This focused, repeated play builds the architecture of focus, attention, goal setting, and more. All of this points to the idea that the limbic system, as the seat of emotions, is the gatekeeper of engagement and interest—and the gateway to learning!

## SUPPORTING PLAY INTERESTS AND CHOICE

You don't have to do anything to unleash play. In fact, you can go anywhere in the world and witness children harnessing play purely through their beautiful, innate instinct to do so. We all have access to this incredible force of nature through all stages of life. It drives infants to roll over, crawl, pull up on tables, and ultimately walk. Play drives development. Play is the most powerful force on the planet. It has taken us to the moon and developed electric cars and artificial intelligence. Play drives innovation. It is our access to being fully self-realized. When we don't play, we don't develop.

Recently, I was walking in Paris, past a playground full of children playing. The sounds of the play could have been happening in Beijing, China; Rotterdam, the Netherlands; or Tulsa, Oklahoma. The truth is that all children are wired for play.

Play is one of the universal drives inherent in human nature, and children are born knowing how to do it:

- A three-month-old baby sees an object of interest and follows it with their eyes.
- A six-month-old baby sees an object of interest and reaches for it.
- A nine-month-old baby holds an object of interest and passes it back and forth from one hand to another.
- A twelve-month-old baby sees an object of interest and crawls to it or pulls up to a coffee table to grab it.

We intuitively understand that babies' interests are driving the development of fine- and gross-motor skills. We delight in their delight. What I find so fascinating is that we abandon this notion as young children become more articulate. Why is a four-year-old's interest in play no longer important? Why are we asking kindergarteners to sit still in their chairs and listen without becoming restless? Where on earth did we get the idea that worksheets are better for a budding mind than play?

I hear some of you saying that a four-year-old can count, whereas a three-month-old cannot. This is true, but does it mean that children's interests should be ignored? The truth is that play develops a child's physical, emotional, and mental growth. If you observe children at play, you can see their cognitive development in motion, and you can observe how their individual developmental needs are served by their unique interests.

A four-year-old sees a peg in Styrofoam, picks up a mallet, and pounds it deep into it. A fascination with force arises out of an interest in play. Perhaps this child is a future carpenter or furniture maker. A five-year-old is obsessed with superheroes. She goes to the art center to create a superhero shield. A love of designing and constructing play props arises out of an interest she expressed through play. Maybe we'll see this child's artfully crafted sets on Broadway in twenty years. A six-year-old is deeply fascinated by insects. He asks his teacher for a blank book so he can write and illustrate a book for his friends. A passion for writing arises out of this play interest. Will this child someday become a published author whose words change lives? In these examples, we see the wonder and potential for nurturing children's brilliance. We don't know exactly how children's play interests will someday translate into the contributions they'll make to the world, but we can be the springboard that provides them with every opportunity to pursue what makes them special and unique.

As early childhood educators, we must make learning personally relevant to students so that the very act of learning excites their emotions. This sets the stage for a natural drive to learn and provides children with the big brain chemical rewards we've discussed that keep them coming back for more. These rewards make children's learning permanent and encourage the development of their innate intelligence. And the most personally relevant curriculum we can give our students is interest-driven, play-based learning.

As previously outlined, the traditional approach to young children was to train them to sit, do as they're told, and no matter what, be compliant! Many centers and schools still reflect values that hail from a time when educators didn't understand how the human brain develops. Current brain research tells us that to properly prepare children for academic learning, they need to actively participate in their learning. Allowing them freedom of choice is the first touchpoint (Goldberg 2022).

When we first give children choices, things can get messy. Most children haven't been given the opportunity to execute choice. It's new and unfamiliar territory for them. Instead, many children have been given passive experiences involving things like computers, touch screens, and toys with predetermined outcomes, essentially having choices made for them. It only makes sense that when we first allow them the capacity to choose, some children will struggle, particularly children who are neurodiverse.

How do we as educators help children who are having difficulty with choice? We know one of the best ways to support children is through their interests, because at this level, we're homing in on what matters to them and what is meaningful to them. This is not a cookie-cutter approach. Each child's journey is unique, and engaging them when a barrier exists can be a process in and of itself. One of the best ways to tap into children's interests is through the lens of play schemas and urges. In my experience, play drives development when children are highly focused on a specific play urge or big idea. It's the breadcrumbs of development! In my educational practice, I like to recognize and support those interests to keep the goodness going.

## OFFERING PLAY INVITATIONS

A learning environment based on wonder creates the foundation for the future of every child in your care. I like to build wonder by offering play invitations. Play invitations offer us a rich opportunity as educators not only to acknowledge the interests of children but to honor them. They bridge our observations of children's unique motivations and interests with practical ways to nurture and encourage their innate intelligence by offering opportunities for further exploration. A play invitation is not a predetermined curriculum imposed regardless of what children express through play, but rather an intentionally crafted way to build on children's naturally occurring curiosity and interests to lay a foundation for future learning opportunities. With that context in mind, let's take a look at what a play invitation actually looks like.

A play invitation is a thoughtful arrangement of materials in the environment designed to spark interest, curiosity, and child-directed play. Rather than prescribing specific activities, you create an invitation by selecting open-ended materials and presenting them in an intriguing manner. The goal is to spark interest.

A play invitation is not a topic or a theme. Children's interests are more than a topic, and physical actions are as important as materials. Think verb, not noun. What actions do you see the children engaged in? Provide a play invitation that builds on that action.

A mindset that has served me well is to be a researcher of children's play. I notice children playing and test my own ideas and theories about what is engaging them in play by setting up play invitations.

To illustrate this point, I observed a child playing with playdough—mainly alone—in the home living area for ninety minutes. One of my priorities in preparing play invitations is to spark social play, so I set up a food-making center there. As a result, children gathered alongside one another, including the child whose initial interest I had followed, and participated in shared play. They created "meals" together and took on roles such as "head cook" and "food deliverer." They shared cooking utensils and communicated with one another about things like what kinds of meals they should prepare and what their favorite foods were. Needless to say, it brought the children together beautifully.

If the play invitation I set up does not engage the children, it gives me valuable feedback that I have not quite tapped into what is capturing their interest. Failed play invitations are certain to happen—you're testing your ideas!

I've found the most engaging play invitations have two key traits:

- Open-ended: A powerful play invitation is open-ended. There is no finished product or outcome, and the children decide where to take the invitation.
- Built upon interest: A great play invitation is built upon existing play interests noticed in the environment. It's taking an interest observed and bringing it to life.

## NOTICING CHILDREN'S MOTIVATIONS

When we're noticing what children at play are doing, we want to examine their motivations. The intensity of motivation that children naturally bring to play creates neural pathways of attention and focus. This is preparing young children for academic settings and future learning.

How do we observe children's play motivations? There are two simple methods of identifying these: (1) considering the play urges and (2) considering the big ideas in play.

### Considering the Play Urges

In her book *Extending Thought in Young Children: A Parent-Teacher Partnership*, Chris Athey introduced the idea of schema theory. Athey defines schemas as "a pattern of repeatable behaviour into which experiences are assimilated and that are gradually co-ordinated" (50).

Others, like Penni Brownlee and Kimberley Crisp, two early childhood thought leaders from New Zealand, have called schemas play urges (Brownlee 2016). In my own practice, this helped me see and identify what I saw as children played: impulsive urges that arise in children as they play. When I see repeated actions in play, I know I'm tapping into a play motivation.

Deb Curtis and Nadia Jaboneta (2019) identified eight common schemas we see in young children:

| SCHEMA | DEFINITION | OBSERVABLE PLAY URGES | |
|---|---|---|---|
| **Transporting** | Moving items from one place to another, often with a container. | Gathering/Collecting<br>Hoarding<br>Carrying<br>Distributing/Parceling Out | Dumping<br>Hauling/Lugging<br>Scattering |
| **Connecting/ Disconnecting** | Joining objects together and taking them apart. | Connecting/Linking<br>Attaching<br>Constructing/Building<br>Stacking | Nesting<br>Sticking<br>Fastening |
| **Trajectory** | Exploring movement of objects or their own body. | Throwing/Tossing<br>Chasing/Running<br>Rolling<br>Jumping/Hopping/ Climbing | Bouncing<br>Dropping<br>Knocking Down<br>Pushing/Pulling |
| **Positioning and Ordering** | Actively noticing similarities and differences, sorting and classifying by creating lines, patterns, and groups | Ordering<br>Lining Up<br>Sorting/Grouping<br>Sequencing | Creating Repeating Patterns<br>Stacking<br>Classifying<br>Balancing |
| **Enclosure/ Containing** | Creating boundaries or containing objects or oneself. | Enclosing<br>Encircling<br>Fencing in | Barricading<br>Creating Entrances/Exits<br>Tunneling |
| **Transforming** | Exploring changes in substances. | Mixing/Stirring<br>Blending/Whisking<br>Pouring | Squishing<br>Squeezing<br>Beating |
| **Orientation and Perspective** | Exploring diverse perspectives by physically manipulating their viewpoints and surroundings. | Rotating<br>Balancing<br>Swinging | Hanging Upside Down<br>Sliding<br>Climbing for Height |
| **Rotation and Circularity** | Exploring rotational movement and circular forms. | Spinning<br>Twirling<br>Twisting | Rolling<br>Dancing in Circles<br>Turning |

Another simple way to begin to see the play urges that are engaging for our children is to use the "follow the verb" method. In looking at what captures children's interests, we want to think in terms of verbs, not nouns. The focus is less on the things of interest, although these do give us valuable clues, but rather on what's happening within their world of play and exploration. Check out the Follow the Verb Checklist in appendix B on page 155.

One year I had a child who just sat watching and would not engage. I asked his parents about what he enjoyed at home, and they told me he loved train sets. The seemingly obvious thing to do would have been to fill the room with books on trains and put out a train set or two.

In my Waldorf training, we learned that at this young age, children are really in their physicality and the concreteness of that physicality. This is, in part, why we consider the actions (verbs) we're observing as our primary clues versus the objects (nouns) involved. Instead of looking for books about trains, I began to follow a thread by asking myself questions: "Okay, if we have a train set, and he loves train sets, what is it that he is doing with that train set? What is the physicality of that? He's moving the trains, he's racing the trains, he's hitching them together. He's hooking the pieces to one another, attaching the track, and enclosing it." As I followed that thread, some play urges began to be revealed.

Instead of thinking about the noun *train*, I considered the verbs involved in playing with a train set:

- *attaching*
- *moving*
- *hooking*
- *turning*
- *enclosing*

I took these verbs and began to test ideas I had about what play urge was driving his play. In every photo his mother shared with me, he had built the train track around himself so he was enclosed. This sparked an idea to set up a play invitation with a variety of medium-sized boxes and a Waldorf trifold play stand that he could use to build an enclosure. The first day I put this out, he built three different structures enclosing himself. In the next iteration, I added fabric for tent making.

To truly understand the schema being presented by children, I next consider what is capturing their interest the most. Again, we can ask ourselves: "Which actions are they repeating?" Once you've had your aha moment and have discovered what actions are at the heart of the child's play, you now have the ingredients for planning accordingly. This will inform the choices you make in offering engaging provocations and creating a setting in which executive functioning can blossom and thrive.

## Considering the Big Play Ideas in Play

"Big play ideas" are a way to organize what you observe in children's narratives. They're a lens for looking for the broad brushstrokes of ideas and topics the children are talking about as they're playing. Big play ideas are ideas children play with, like playing with blocks, and they'll show up in many ways and forms. Diane Kashin (2023) said it best, "Big ideas refer to concepts that are meaningful to the lives of children." Building on the previous example, trains are a topic, whereas speed is a big idea. As an educator, I can facilitate children's exploration and discovery of speed across multiple areas of the classroom.

The following are other big play ideas I've seen play out in my education practice.

### *Lines*

A group of children in my pre-K classroom were making long marks. Here are a few ways I took the concept of line into extended experiences:

- We followed the lines down the hallway on the floor of the school.
- We created lines with flashlights.
- We created lines with wire.
- We created a line out of Popsicle sticks from one end of the school building to the other.

### *Sound*

A group of children in my pre-K class were having a "who can be loudest" contest during playtime. It persisted day after day, so I built experiences around it:

- We created a loud band outside.

- We made a yelling tent on the playground.
- We took sound walks to listen for what we heard.
- We used drums to explore their volume range.
- We made our own drums.

Looking at play from the big play ideas mindset can expand what's possible and lead to deeper and more profound projects and investigations. Adopting this mindset empowers us as educators to understand and expand on the child's perspective. It gives us the capacity to provoke deeper understandings that are united in an overarching idea.

## NOTICING IN PRACTICE

When we address children at a heart level, we tend to the deepest part of them—their passion. One of the most powerful practices for responding to children's passions is what my friend and colleague Lynnette Arthur calls "noticings." Noticing is tuning into children's interests, conversations, and behaviors. You might be wondering how noticing is different from observation. Observation is typically an objective point of view, aimed at gathering information, usually with a specific goal or application in mind. Noticing is subjective. It is observation through the eyes of a deeply attached and thoughtful educator with an intent to truly see the individual and understand their perspective and experience.

In 2004 I taught a four-year-old class. Many of the children walked to school with their moms and dogs. One day Amelia, a tiny girl with pale skin and dark brown hair down to her shoulders, came to me in tears.

"Mrs. Haughey, my mom will never let me have a pet." She was devastated.

A few days later, she arrived at school excited and full of glee. "Mrs. Haughey! Mrs. Haughey! At group meeting time I have a very special show and share!"

At group time, I asked Amelia to tell us about her special show and share. Amelia went to her cubby and pulled out a large matchbox. She slowly pulled out the drawer and revealed a big fat worm on a gently folded tissue. Amelia beamed, "Meet Willy the Worm! My pet worm." Her joy was palpable, not only in how she presented her new, beloved pet to the class but also in the ways she had tended to Willy's every need. I noticed how Amelia brought care to every moment of Willy's visit. He had a bed, a tiny TV, and even a little hairbrush. Everything Amelia did that day, Willy did too.

The following Monday, Amelia arrived at school in tears. "What's wrong Amelia?"

Big tears dropped from her eyes. "Mrs. Haughey, I found out that worms need water. Willy is dead."

I gave her a hug. I could see she was deeply saddened, and we sat together in her loss. Searching for a way to help Amelia process this sad event, I asked if she might like to research with me and find out how to raise and care for worms.

That turn of events launched a three-month study of worms and the installation of a large worm farm in our program. Amelia was playing with the idea of having a pet (and the big idea of care) and searching for a way to meet the interest she felt in having one. Following her passion led us to a deep and powerful study. It paved the way for learning and experiential growth that all of the children in the classroom benefited from, as did our garden with the beautifully aerated dirt we were able to offer it.

Today many teachers have far too much pressure to achieve benchmarks to allow for this kind of nurturing of children's souls. Tending to Amelia's heart was not driven by data but rather by noticing and honoring her huge interest in caring for a pet. Her limbic system was switched on around anything regarding pets, and her execution of choice in finding one in Willy is a beautiful illustration of what can take place when we follow children's innate interests.

In the practice of noticing, we watch for children struggling in play. Observing children provides clues to help us help them fully engage. What about children who go from activity to activity without really engaging? Are they able to immerse themselves in an exploration for the joy and pleasure of it? They dabble and wander from one place to another. How do we support them in exploring and experimenting?

I have discovered that the most important noticing strategy is listening deeply to what the children are saying and doing. As educators, we want to be researchers. What is engaging them? How quickly does it stop? What is their disposition? What repeated patterns are showing up? I use a Daily Reflection Form (find it in the appendix) to help capture patterns and dispositions that stand out each day.

Additionally, something I developed in my practice when I was in academic-pressured environments in public school was a whole collection of noticing forms to help me observe and assess play directly. These forms included the different types of play, such as the developmental use of loose parts and the developmental sequence of playing with clay. You will find my forms Developmental Stages of Block Play and Developmental Stages of Loose Parts Play in appendix B. Depending on your setting, and whether it's through more "formal" assessment or your own method of observation and note-taking, I highly encourage you to gather this kind of information about the children in your care. The time and effort you spend doing so will yield some of the most precious, valuable insights you could hope for when it comes to nurturing their brilliance and setting the stage for future learning.

## LET THE CHILDREN LEAD

Considering the information we've covered in this chapter, my hope is that you'll take the following to heart and incorporate it into your own play-based practice: *If we allow them, children can be their own champions of their growth and development.*

The "answers" lie within the children and their play. By following the trail of their interests and how they engage with them—how they play with them—we're handed the information we need to create settings and opportunities that foster children's growth and development. Our eyes, ears, and hearts are our most valuable tools in this precious work. Now that you've been empowered with more insight, information, and understanding about the interests of children, my hope is that you'll now view those—as well as the multitude of opportunities they present for our best work with children—through a new and clearer lens.

I conclude this chapter with an illustration of how following the lead of children's play and interests—and supporting their choices—can not only inform our practice but our souls as well:

> "Mrs. Haughey! It's not fair! Make them stop!"
>
> A group of seven or eight children are packed tightly into the dramatic play area, which is under a play stand draped with silk. We've just finished a four-week investigation into the fairy tale "Goldilocks and the Three Bears," and I had put wooden bowls of all kinds in the dramatic play center, including a large one with a lid.
>
> Three children are fighting to gain control over the bowl.

"Mrs. Haughey," says Malik, a small boy with dark eyes and a huge smile, "Let's act it out!"

One of the strategies I use at the beginning of school is to role-play and act out difficult moments. The children want to reenact the conflict.

It doesn't take long before the entire class wants to take part. Twenty children are acting out three roles. It's a wild moment to be sure, and I could have said no. But my mantra is to trust the process of the children. The children act it out and we gather on the carpet.

"Mrs. Haughey, we need to be peacekeepers," Malik says with excitement. He's had a revelation of sorts, and it shows on his beaming face.

Martin Luther King Day had been only a few weeks earlier. Malik smiles. "We need to be more like Dr. King."

That day, twenty four-year-olds talked about what it means to solve problems with words and peace. Beginning with one of the most common and age-old phenomena known to humankind—conflict—we followed the trail of their interests and set the stage for something beautiful and wonder-filled to unfold. These children harnessed the power of play that day to arrive at a strategy for moving forward together as a group of human beings driven by a passion for peace. Pure brilliance. We have so much to learn from children.

> *Aha Note!*
>
> The intensity of motivation that children naturally bring to play creates neural pathways of attention and focus.

## GOLD NUGGETS

- Consider this: Children are not born with executive function, yet in play, they can sustain their focus for long periods. When children choose their play, they are more likely to become highly focused because it's important.
- Play drives interest. It drives development. Play is the most powerful force on the planet. It has taken us to the moon and developed electric cars and artificial intelligence. Play drives innovation. It is our access to being fully self-realized.

## THE PRACTICE OF THE EDUCATOR: NOTICING

The most important aspect of this pillar is children's agency in having choice. This is the magic ingredient of play. If choice does not exist, then play does not exist. Several mindset practices have helped me overcome the deep hold of my own upbringing of compliance.

### Practice 1: Noticing Joy

Early in my career, I noticed something important. Sometimes children at play get deep into something that gives them a primal satisfaction. In these moments, the children's attention in play lasts for a long time. A state of joy is evident. I call this following the breadcrumbs of joy. Noticing and following this primal satisfaction, or joy, is how you can support what really matters to children. True joy is a profoundly calming experience. Side note: When you see children in joy while creating destruction and chaos, it's an opportunity for you to help them find ways of expressing that joy in ways that work—not a time for behavior management or shutting down the play.

### Practice 2: Noticing the Emotional Drivers in Play

Recognizing and honoring the children's emotional needs is where I found the most powerful and life-changing play projects. When you put the four pillars into practice, you will begin to witness how children are bringing their emotional needs to their play, like Claire's need to write to the turtles. I call this Observing from the Heart.

I learned a secret practice in my Waldorf training that has helped me observe the children in my care in this way—from my heart. Every night before I go to sleep, I picture each child in my class. I picture the color of their hair, their eyes, and their general disposition. As I gain skill in my recall abilities, I begin remembering what they were wearing that day. For example, I might try to remember the color of their shoes.

This practice is nothing short of a miracle. It creates a connection with each child that provides intuitive knowledge about them. Often, through this deep connection, I could read dispositions before behaviors showed up. I would know on sight when a child was getting sick. This practice has always helped me tap into the emotional needs that sit underneath play and has been a deep and powerful way that I observe and notice the children in my care.

CHAPTER 5

# REPETITION

So often I hear adults saying, well, how do we motivate children to learn? Oh, you do not have to motivate children to learn. They are driven to master the world around them, and, you know, they do that through repetition.

—Rebecca Parlakian

## Repetition Pillar

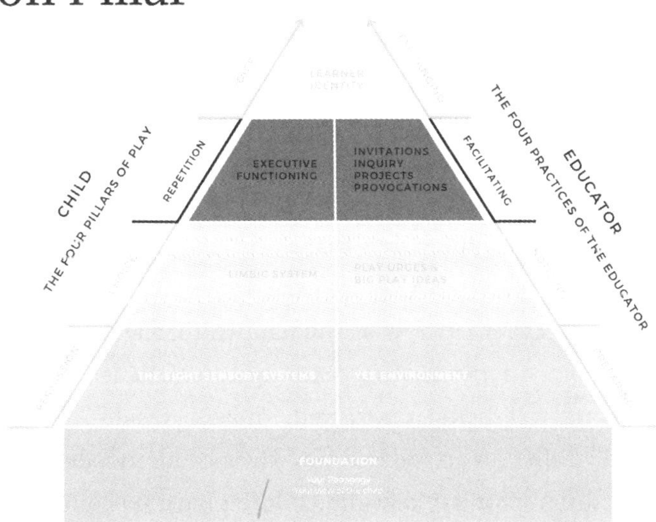


As a grandmother and a preschool educator, I've witnessed firsthand how the joy of repetitive play can shape a child's development. Once my seven-year-old grandson, Kam, transformed his upstairs playroom into a pretend restaurant that consisted of two pretend kitchen sets, a kid-coffee machine, artificial food, and menus. When I arrived at the top of the stairs, I noticed a cash register.

"Welcome!" Kam greeted me. "It costs ten dollars to enter."

I handed him a strip of paper—our makeshift currency—and he gestured for me to take a seat. Settling onto the couch, I was soon handed a handwritten menu, the product of Kam's efforts.

"What would you like to eat?" he asked, poised with a ticket pad in hand.

"An egg, pineapple, and a hot coffee, please."

With a scribble on his pad, he was off to "prepare" my order.

Once I had finished my pretend meal, Kam turned to me with the words I'd come to anticipate: "Let's do it again." And so we did. I cannot tell you how many times I've "dined" at Kam's restaurant—easily fifty times, perhaps more.

Kam was engaged in one of the most powerful aspects of play—repetition. If we consider this more closely, repetition happens in play because it's fun, pleasurable, and deeply satisfying. For children, continuously revisiting the same play activity is a function of profound connection and meaningful engagement. It is often social, as in Kam's restaurant, bringing together elements of interaction, communication, role-playing, and *brilliance*.

## SECURITY AND REPETITION IN CHILD DEVELOPMENT

If we're going to talk about the power and importance of repetition for young children, we must first acknowledge that the heart of repetition is security. Repetition and routine give children a secure base from which to explore the environment. When children can predict what will happen throughout their day, trust is built! Through repeated activities that occur in a predictable sequence, children's sense of security and well-being is nurtured. Knowing what to expect and knowing that the day will unfold in an ordered way gives children a deep sense of ease. When things are different every day and children have no control over what or where they play, they may feel unsettled or even confused or disturbed.

Routines define children's daily lives. A stable routine provides security because children can both rely on it and come to anticipate it. Routines also help create a rich environment for play and the learning that ensues from it. For example, if a child visits the art center every day, they develop a physical familiarity with the space, acquire dexterity with the materials, gain insights into how paint colors and textures interact, and learn about the social dynamics of working alongside others.

Our best days have both rhythm and routine:

| RHYTHM | ROUTINE |
|---|---|
| **Rhythm refers to the flow, pacing, and timing of the day.**<br>Rhythm is felt in the regular patterns that give a sense of continuity and beat to the schedule and activities. Here are some examples of rhythm in an early childhood setting:<br>• Holding daily events at consistent times (arrival, circle time, outside play, and so forth)<br>• Regularly alternating active and calm times (free play followed by cleanup followed by story time)<br>• Using songs/chants during transitions such as a cleanup song<br>• Repeating themes/projects over days or weeks, such as an in-depth study of butterflies | **Routines follow steps in a defined procedure.**<br>Routines refer to specific, repeating sequences of events or behaviors. They are the set procedures and patterns that structure the day. Here are some examples of routines in an early childhood setting:<br>• Morning arrival routine (put backpack away, mark attendance on chart, start choice time)<br>• Snacktime routine (wash hands, sit at table, serve snack family style, scrape plate when done)<br>• Cleanup routine (sing cleanup song, put toys in proper bins, push in chairs, meet on rug)<br>• End-of-day routine (pack backpack, put on coats, line up to go outside) |

Rhythm and routine help children find self-regulation. When children can anticipate activities, they learn to monitor their own behaviors and emotions.

The foundation of a highly effective play environment is a predictable setting where children feel safe and secure. Repetition supports young children at the place where they are developmentally. Important to note is that this ability to thrive through repetition depends largely on the relationship and attention children receive from their primary caregivers. They need to see and feel the interest and delight their caregivers take in their play. This interactive and supportive relationship reinforces their sense of security and further enhances the richness of their play experiences.

Inside a repeating daily schedule, a child's freedom of choice becomes the holy grail of play-based education. When we take away their right to choose where they play, we are taking away from children's innate drive to grow and develop. In the second pillar of the Play-Activated Learning (PAL) model, Choice, children are following their own interests in play. Repetition cannot occur until we allow children to engage in what is personally interesting to them. A child who returns daily to play in the blocks area is clearly finding satisfaction and pleasure in that activity.

When we engage in a personal interest, we're pursuing pleasure. I love watercolor painting, and some Saturdays I find myself ignoring mealtimes until I feel complete with my painting experience. Children are no different. They pursue the same form of play until they've reached a level of satisfaction within the experience.

When Liz, my firstborn, started crawling, I was taken aback by the joy she demonstrated in her attempts. She would push herself up on all fours and attempt to move forward. She did this over and over. One day, while rocking on all fours, she moved, full infant-steam ahead, by inches. She squealed with delight. Gradually, she began moving a bit more, and then some more, until she was fully capable of crawling. Her success in crawling required intense repetition to achieve. She wasn't able to crawl immediately, and, of course, she failed time and again. The excitement and drive she exhibited to accomplish this milestone was awe-inspiring! As it was with Liz, the progression from crawling to walking is an exhilarating achievement for any young child.

Play is a deeply satisfying experience by design, and repetition plays a role in this. Through continuously revisiting this profound sense of joy and satisfaction, the good stuff arises. Think back to the limbic system and the reward loop we discussed in the previous chapter. Play is pleasurable, and because of that, children will repeat activities they enjoy, and they are more likely to remember and learn from their repetitive behaviors. As Douglas Hintzman (1976) discovered in his research, repetition is one of the most powerful variables affecting memory.

## BUILDING NEURAL CONNECTIONS THROUGH PLAY

My grandmother used to say that a child's brain is like a sponge, ready to be filled with new information, so I'd better listen well! Despite this well-seasoned wisdom, however, our current understanding of neuroscience paints a more complex picture. Instead of a sponge, envision a child's brain as an intricate network of airports, with each airport symbolizing a neuron waiting to be linked with other neurons via information pathways, or "flight paths," known as neural bridges.

Unfortunately, most public schools still adhere to the "sponge method" of brain growth, often at the expense of play-based learning. Play is being removed from early childhood settings worldwide because of a mistaken belief that we should prepare children for school as much as we can and as early as we can. Programs that promote teaching preschool children reading and math are founded on this "sponge" perspective of brain growth. They ignore what we know and what the science tells us about play and repetition.

Consider again the child who gravitates toward the art center at school. Each day, they return to this area to engage in the creative activities they love. Each time, the neural bridges are strengthened in relation to that repeated experience of "playing in the art center," each time strengthening the child's intelligence and development. Let me emphasize: *Repetition is the foundation of building intelligence.* Let's look closer at what's happening on a neurological level when children repeat activities.

Neurons that are frequently used develop on their axons a multilayered covering known as myelin. The axon is the portion of a nerve cell (neuron) that carries impulses away from it. This sheath, myelin, accelerates nerve impulse transmission. When we first learn something, the process is slow, like making a path through a grassy field. Initially, there's no clear pathway. As you walk that way again and again, a pathway forms, just like when the myelin is laid down when our neurons are used over and over. The more myelin is formed, the faster the transmission becomes. Over time, the pathway evolves into a well-paved highway, where information travels at high speed, making tasks feel easy and almost automatic. Activities that become seemingly effortless and practically second nature to us, like brushing our teeth or riding a bike, are good examples of this.

Think about the child who asks you to read a book again and again. This repetition allows them to myelinate new nerve pathways. Every time an action is repeated, neural connections are being reinforced. This process was clearly demonstrated by my son, Ben, when he was beginning to learn to play the cello. He played the scales daily. At first, it sounded like squawking and squeaking, until one day, the most amazing sound came from his instrument.

It took Ben hundreds of hours to master playing the scales. With repetition, the brain begins to understand and master tasks, and these neural pathways become permanent. For adults, many of these neural connections are well established. We can drive cars, brew coffee, and perform numerous tasks thanks to our past experiences. However, children are just beginning to form these neural connections, and repetition is the key to this process.

As Judith Wright, codirector of the London Suzuki Music Centre in Ontario, points out, "A baby needs 1,000 repetitions to learn a word; by the time he's a toddler, he might need fifty repetitions; and when he's in kindergarten, he may need only a few repetitions to master it because the brain connections have been laid out" (Kryczka 2021). Harvard neuroscientist Charles Nelson III states that brain wiring is made possible by repetition: "If you have a whole group of neurons that have to start to develop into a circuit, they need to be fired over and over. Neurons that fire together, wire together" (Chatterjee 2024) .

The process of nerve cells connecting and networking is the fabric of learning. Children develop their neural pathways in response to their life experiences. A major component of experience is sensory input from our environment through our eight sensory systems. Our whole body is a fine-tuned sensory receptor, collecting information to facilitate learning and development. When the limbic system and reward pathways are fully engaged in this process, as they are in play (versus unchosen, teacher-led activities like worksheets and templatized stations), the stage is now set for optimal learning and the integration of new skills.

## REPETITION AND THE FREEDOM TO CHOOSE

In the third pillar of the PAL model, Repetition, seeing repeating activities indicates that the children are actively planning their play. They're walking into the room and thinking on some level, "Okay, I'm going to play with blocks." Then, the next day, they walk in, again thinking, "Okay, I'm going to play with blocks." The child is consciously choosing their activity. It's as if they are following an internal compass that guides them to the same activity daily. This clear and definite preference is not a sign of monotony or a lack of inspiration or creativity on the child's part. What may appear to be random and unintentional is nature's brilliant design in action.

Children's repetition of specific activities over and over builds sustained focus and attention, laying a solid foundation for executive functioning. Unfortunately, there is a widespread practice among early childhood educators worldwide to rotate children through centers, preventing this kind of focused repetition. This approach, while well-intentioned, overlooks the immense learning opportunities that repetition offers. It's like asking a budding musician to switch instruments every day; the depth of skill and understanding that comes from focused practice is lost.

Lev Vygotsky, a renowned Russian and Soviet psychologist, emphasized the value of repeated experiences in his teachings. He suggested that children learn to plan their activities through these repeated experiences. Consider a child repeatedly building towers with blocks. With each new tower, they are not merely repeating the same activity but advancing to a higher level, much like a stairway in which each step is similar but elevates them to a new height. Repetition lets young children learn skills in a progression of development by building on past experiences. The similarities found in a prior experience can be accessed when relating to a new experience, and prior learning is carried forward into new experiences and learned skills.

It's crucial to support freedom of choice in play, even if children's activities appear senseless or silly to us. Children's play activities are not random; rather, they are of great importance and their repetition plays a vital role. A deeper pattern that drives children's growth and development emerges through this repetition, a pattern that we cannot always detect or observe. The benefit is not always immediately visible, particularly to the well-intended but untrained eyes of administrators and families. This is where the struggle for advocating for play-based education begins.

### WHEN REPETITION MIGHT BE OF CONCERN

While repetition and freedom are vital components of play, they can occasionally lead to unique challenges. Here's how an educator can address these concerns:

- **When children are unable to leave their play to follow the daily rhythm:** If a child is deeply immersed in an activity and struggles to transition to the next part of the day, you can provide gentle reminders and countdowns (for example, "In five minutes, we'll need to clean up and get ready for lunch"). Providing visual previews of what's coming as well as visual schedules can help some children immensely. We want to help the child prepare mentally for the transition.
- **When children cannot shift their focus from their play big ideas to the topic of the group:** If a child is absorbed in a specific theme (like dinosaurs) while the class is discussing a different topic (plants), you can try to create a bridge between the child's interest and the group's discussion (for example, "Do you know what plants dinosaurs ate?"). This approach can help engage the child in the group discussion.
- **When a child will only play with a specific person and not anyone else:** If a child prefers to play only with a particular peer, you can encourage interactions with different children through group activities. It's helpful to gather students for interest-specific small groups. In this small setting, it's easier to connect friendships.

As educators, we are to guide and support children's play, ensuring it remains a positive, equitable, and enriching experience for all.

## RESPONDING TO REPETITION

Play holds a sacred space in the landscape of childhood. It's a sanctuary where children can be their true and authentic selves, a space deserving of our respect and honor. When we honor a child's play, we are acknowledging their voice, their identity, and their unique perspective. We are honoring their passions, desires, and intrinsic motivations in play, not ours. We are nurturing the spark of curiosity and joy in their eyes, the same spark that lights the path of their learning journey. In all of these contexts, we are acknowledging, honoring, and nurturing children's innate brilliance.

As educators, we watch children as they explore their play world, noting their interests, their interactions, and their emerging skills. We are empowered to follow the path of repetitive activities and themes that are so vital to children's sense of security, routine, choice, sustained focus, and deep learning. These observations offer insights into the child's unique journey and provide clues as to how we might enrich their explorations by introducing invitations, provocations, projects, and inquiries. The process is fluid and ever evolving. Play changes, morphs, and transforms over time, shaped by relationships and experiences.

Our role is to invite children deeper into their own ideas and thinking. It is a big task to discern the motivations and interests in play that are driving their exploration. Everything we do circles around their play urges and big ideas.

In this cycle of play-activated learning, we're not just educators. We're observers, facilitators, and, most importantly, respectful supporters of each child's unique journey. We're always honoring the child's role as the true captain of their voyage of discovery.

### *The Cycle of Play-Activated Learning*

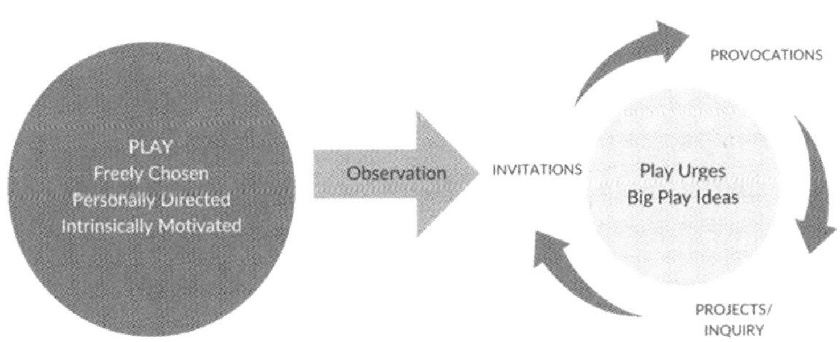


In play-based learning, educators create opportunities for children's exploration. As discussed repeatedly in this book, play should be freely chosen, not imposed. Invitations, provocations, and new materials can enrich play without dictating it.

A **play invitation** or provocation deepens existing play urges. For example, providing additional loose parts that add height to blocks might support the children's urge to build up. A play invitation is an open-ended exploration. There is no predetermined outcome. The children may use the play invitation the way the educator envisioned, or they may take the materials and use them in entirely different ways. In a play invitation, children are not bound by the constraints of the materials they're offered. Instead, a play invitation acts as a launchpad for children's own ideas and theories to develop. (See the Play Invitation Planner in appendix B on page 159 for a helpful framework for doing this.)

A **project or inquiry** allows deeper exploration around a big idea. Through projects, children gain and develop knowledge and skills through investigation and exploration of a single idea. Inquiries are presented in the context of questions or challenges. The initial wondering may lead to new and completely different ideas where a project will stay focused on a single big idea. The "teacher as researcher" mindset helps facilitate this exploration. For example, an inquiry into speed could lead children to explore cars on ramps, marbles on concrete, wheels, and pedaling. Real-life experiences enrich these investigations, making them dynamic and engaging. These inquiries happen when we build an entire deep dive series of invitations and provocations around a big idea or play urge in which we've seen the children actively engaged.

At the heart of an inquiry is a central, overarching concept like speed. What makes a strong concept for an inquiry is first and foremost that it is open-ended. We want to leave space for the children's interests to drive where we will go with the concept. Ideally, we want the central concept to be applicable to any play area. The teacher can bring it to art, nature, blocks, or science centers, to name a few—anything or anywhere at all. Another distinguishing factor of a good concept is that it provides a kaleidoscope of real-life experiences. Children can connect with it from their own experiences because it is found in their everyday lives.

Next, a robust central concept will offer many ways for the children to investigate and explore. These investigations and explorations form the core of a web of possible directions an inquiry can take. These questions within the inquiry help reveal what interests the child, as well as what they already know about the central concept.

An inquiry includes real experiences. This is what makes the inquiry process so dynamic—actual experience with the central concept and inquiry topics. Young children learn best when they've experienced firsthand what they are investigating in a playful way.

From the information we've just covered in this chapter, we can see that repetition in children's play not only sets the stage for deep learning and development but also suggests the directions we take next in our settings. It shines a light on emerging play urges that can then inform the invitations, provocations, and inquiries we offer children. Through our thoughtful observation of repetition, we aren't given a container to work within. Instead, a vast, wonder-filled landscape of possibilities opens up, where children can blossom and thrive. What at first may seem nonsensical, silly, and perhaps odd to many adults and even educators is actually the hallmark of a profound and developmentally powerful stage of learning. It is the emerging of children's brilliance.

> *Aha Note!*
>
> Repetition is the foundation of building intelligence.

### GOLD NUGGETS

- Rhythm and routine help children find self-regulation. When children can anticipate activities, they learn to monitor their own behaviors and emotions.
- Inside a repeating daily schedule, a child's freedom of choice becomes the holy grail of play-based education.
- Our role is to invite children deeper into their own ideas and thinking.

## THE PRACTICE OF THE EDUCATOR: FACILITATING

As play-based educators, we embrace various roles, all with the overarching goal of nurturing children's innate brilliance. We've discussed the role and importance of observation, and through this practice arrive at another equally important practice—facilitation. The assembly line model of education, as we explored earlier in the book, has educators filling children with "knowledge." In play-based education, we do the opposite as we facilitate children's innate intelligence. It might seem counterintuitive, but we can do this by supporting them to struggle.

As they begin to engage in repetitive play, some children come up against the limits of their growing capacities and become frustrated. Often they lash out at their friends and even fall into tantrums.

I noticed early in my career that I was processing these moments as "conflict" and approaching them as such. I found myself intervening in ways that implied something was wrong and needed to be "fixed" with my help, rather than viewing these situations as opportunities for me to facilitate the children's development of prosocial skills and behaviors. My interventions were actually shutting down the potential learning and growth inherent in the situation. Instead, I want to share how I facilitate children in breakdown.

When I first approach a child in breakdown, I sit and help the child come back to calm. I affirm their feelings and offer support. I am a safe harbor first and foremost.

Next, once the child is calm, I assist the child's thwarted efforts.

For example, in my three-year-old class, a little boy named Michael wanted to build a tower larger than himself. Slowly he built the tower to his shoulders. But as he reached this height, his block structure began to fall down, every single time. He would fall on the ground crying and sometimes would kick other children's structures in his upset over his own.

At first, I sat down with Michael and provided support in letting him express his frustration to an understanding ear. But helping him calm himself was not helping solve his problem. The engineering issue was that in building a tower "taller than me," Michael was inadvertently knocking it down every time. Because I wanted him to discover his own solution, I filmed him building a tower so he could see what was happening.

I showed the recording to Michael. "What do you notice?" I asked him.

Michael immediately saw the problem. When his arm went up to place the blocks at shoulder height, his elbow hit the blocks, causing them to tumble.

"How might you solve the problem?" I inquired.

He asked me, "Can I stand on a chair to be tall enough?"

The extra height allowed him to build the block tower and not knock it down. Sometimes children need a little extra help in their struggles to harness their innate intelligence. Michael just needed to be able to see the problem for himself.

CHAPTER 6

# VOICE

Every day, in a hundred small ways, our children ask, "Do you hear me? Do you see me? Do I matter?" Their behavior often reflects our response.

—Attributed to L. R. Knost

## Voice Pillar

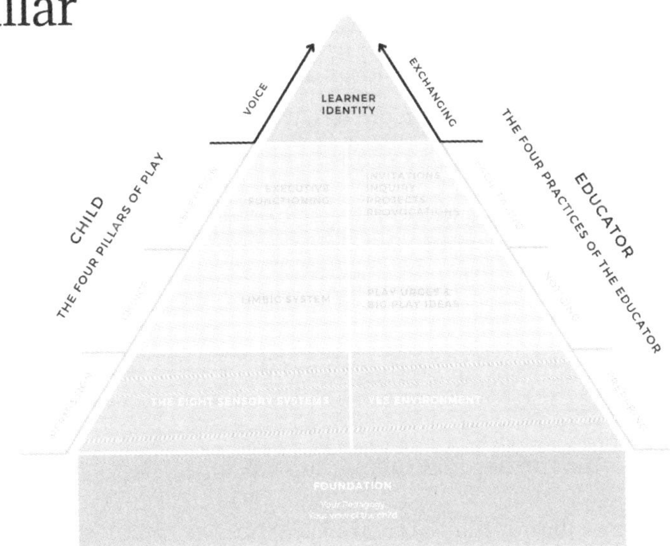


Play is one of the most essential ways children learn to communicate their ideas and find their voice. As we arrive at the fourth pillar of the Play-Activated Learning (PAL) model, we're taking into close consideration how children's voices enable them verbally and nonverbally to thrive as learners. Verbal communication includes speech and vocal sounds. Nonverbal communication includes facial expressions, gestures, and even silences. My most potent teaching moments as an early childhood educator have occurred when children articulate their own perspectives and views. One of the most profound things we can do for our children is to give them a voice that is heard and acted upon.

Giving children a voice begins in infancy. All forms of communication, whether spoken or unspoken, should be valued equally when we are seeking children's perspectives. Recognizing the diverse ways children convey their feelings, ideas, and experiences is critical to elevating their voices. Attention to what children say and communicate through their looks, actions, body language, and behaviors is vital. Appreciating children's varied "languages" demonstrates respect for the many valid ways their voices emerge.

## PASSIVE RECIPIENT VS. ACTIVE PARTICIPANT

To further understand and provide context, let's take a brief look at the child's voice in the traditional setting. As we've previously discussed, the assembly line model of education views children as empty vessels who must be trained into compliant students. Children are passive recipients of teacher-directed education. These are some of the expectations:

- Follows directions without input or questioning (no voice)
- Executes activities and projects to look exactly like the teacher's model (no voice)
- Waits for instruction rather than taking initiative and contributing ideas (no voice)
- Works quietly without talking (no voice)

On the other hand, play-activated learning is about empowering children to be active participants in their education. Children's voices, ideas, theories, and thoughts are central to planning, and they are active participants in the educational process. Here are some of the ways this happens:

- Chooses whether to participate in a process or activity (voice)
- Contributes ideas, asks questions, and provides input (voice)
- Influences setting goals and activities with personal interests (voice)

- Collaborates with others, sharing ideas and interests (voice)

As children develop and language develops, play also develops. Think about it—at first, infants put toys in their mouths to learn how different objects feel and taste through experimentation. Then toddlers play with objects like cars and trucks. While playing, they learn nouns (the names of things like *cars*) and verbs (what objects do or action words like *race*). Play lets children practice their communication skills in a satisfying and comforting setting. Through play, children build the capacity to express their thoughts and ideas while listening and responding to others.

## RECEPTIVE AND EXPRESSIVE LANGUAGE AND LITERACY

Language has two parts: expressive and receptive. Children need both expressive and receptive language skills to communicate effectively with others. The assembly line paradigm strongly supports the receptive language skills of children but falls short of their expressive language needs.

Receptive language is the "input" of language—the ability to understand what is spoken. An example is the ability to follow directions like "Put on your socks and shoes." Receptive language develops before expressive language. For example, you can say to a preverbal toddler, "Pick up the toy," and they will comprehend what you're asking them to do. They won't have the language—yet—to respond to you, but they can understand and assimilate what you've said. Think of a child's receptive language skills as their comprehension of language.

Expressive language—the "output" of language—is the ability to express thoughts, feelings, and desires through verbal and nonverbal communication. Facial expressions, gestures, and eye contact all communicate, even more so than words do at times.

In free play, children make requests and express wants. One of the major markers of play-activated learning is the power wielded by the child's ideas and interests. The child's voice is crucial to what happens in the learning setting. The educators observe and document daily what the children are expressing through play. This observation, and the information it provides, are the heart and soul of the play-based curriculum.

The foundation of literacy rests in the young child's voice. Research has shown that speaking and listening are integral to writing and reading (Lervåg et al. 2017). It is through conversing that children learn new words and expand their vocabulary. A rich exposure to conversations with attentive caregivers provides an invaluable start for children as they build literacy skills.

Two crucial areas underpin a child's growing reading capacity. First is the outer mechanical element of reading, which is the ability to decode the symbols that stand for sounds and words. Most educators focus on this by teaching phonics and phonemic awareness.

Reading has a second area of development rarely discussed—the inner activity of making meaning. It is through a play-rich environment that we can build the inner life of the reader by listening, comprehending, and imagining. When children are given the opportunity to play, building on their own ideas and theories, they are learning to make connections and give meaning to the process of playing.

## A CHILD'S RIGHT TO VOICE

Children develop with their own innate, naturally occurring voices. When children's voices are valued, their opinions, feelings, thoughts, and preferences are heard and incorporated into decisions affecting their lives. As a result, we support their emerging identity and nurture their innate intelligences. Conversations with children make them feel seen, heard, and valued. Giving children opportunities to express themselves and be heard demonstrates respect for their ideas. It communicates in a meaningful and lasting way: *Your ideas matter, and so do you.*

Children have three distinct rights surrounding their voice: to be seen, to be heard, and to be valued. Yet traditional early childhood education allows little to no opportunity for the child's ideas, opinions, and views to be shared. We are still fighting the outdated adage that children should be seen and not heard. Often, educational themes are predetermined and not based in observation, rotation among centers is timed to the needs of the classroom schedule versus children's level of engagement, and activity groups are chosen by the adults. If voicing your ideas, theories, and views develops your identity and sense of self as a learner, where do you get to do this in a traditional early childhood setting?

The United Nations Convention on the Rights of the Child is an international human rights treaty with fifty-four articles that support and advocate the rights of each child. Article 12 advocates for the child's voice:

> Parties shall assure the child who is capable of forming his or her own views the right to express those views freely in all matters affecting the child, the views of the child being given due weight in accordance with the age and maturity of the child. (United Nations General Assembly 1989, pt. 1, art. 12)

This article advocates for each child's right to form views and to be heard. Elevating children's voices means recognizing and listening to their meaningful perspectives and input about issues that affect them.

As educators, we encounter times in which we're called to listen—and observe—even more closely than usual to find opportunities to honor children's voices. This could be for any number of reasons, such as supporting a child who is naturally quiet and soft-spoken. In other cases, children may have already been conditioned not to be heard, and therefore their cues, both verbal and nonverbal, may be harder to detect. And sometimes it may simply be a matter of unfamiliarity with the child in front of us. In any of these circumstances, our task as educators is twofold: to remember that all children have a voice and to find opportunities to nurture it to foster a deeper understanding of them and their interests.

In my own teaching practice, I experienced firsthand the power of a child's voice in setting the stage to thrive in a new and anxiety-inducing environment, as illustrated in the following story about Hayden.

> "Mom! Don't leave me! Take me with you!"
>
> It was January 2013 in Tulsa, Oklahoma, and I was teaching twenty children in a universal pre-K classroom. Hayden had come to my classroom midyear, and it was immediately apparent that he was struggling with the transition to his new classroom.
>
> Every day without fail, Hayden clung to his mother, begging her not to leave him. She would leave and Hayden would cling to a chair, watching the children and the class activities while crying. For hours. Every day.
>
> One day as Hayden arrived, he was talking to his mother about race cars. His eyes were bright, and he was talking with such excitement and enthusiasm. I hadn't seen or heard anything like this from him before. Surely there was something here. Again, he started to cry when his mother left the classroom.

> During free play, I turned on a video playing the Indy 500. Hayden's eyes lit up immediately. "Mrs. Haughey, do you watch car races?"
>
> "No," I answered, "But I heard you talking about it with your mom, and I wanted to know more. Can you tell me about it?" Hayden explained in eager detail who each driver was and how cool the cars were. I pulled out some matchbox cars from storage and placed them in the block center.
>
> Within a matter of minutes, Hayden was playing with his new friends, his classmates who had joined him in play. Within a week, he was running into the classroom, barely saying goodbye to his mother in his zest to play with the Matchbox cars and his companions. This was such a welcome sight instead of his tears! Over the course of the following two weeks during free play, I could find Hayden with the Matchbox cars and his friends day in and day out.
>
> As I watched the scenes unfold each day, I observed signposts as Hayden settled in and flourished in his new setting. I was watching his brilliance unfold. For example, he built a large race car out of blocks, and his new friends piled on behind him as he "drove" fast and furious. Within the following couple of weeks, Hayden was leading his classmates in building their own cars out of pinewood derby kits and hosting a full-blown Grand Prix race. His passion was capturing the hearts of his peers, and it was all built on his deep and repeated interest in cars—an interest that was revealed by listening to him and observing his voice.

Hayden progressed from clinging to a chair to being the most prominent leader in the classroom. I asked myself: "What was it that had helped Hayden finally connect and feel belongingness? What was it that created a bridge for him to engage in classroom activities?"

No textbook, no benchmark, and no standard had helped Hayden. Comforting him and encouraging him had been ineffective. In fact, *nothing* had worked until I found an opportunity to hear his voice, hooked into his interests, and provided a context for play that aligned with his deepest passion.

Hayden's voice offered me a way into his world and interests, with repetition as the bridge. An invitation into play paved the way for him to thrive as a brilliant student, friend, and leader.

## THE POWER OF CONVERSATIONS

In a 1995 landmark study, researchers found that children from families with higher incomes hear about thirty million more words by age three than children from families with lower incomes. This "30 million word gap" was identified as a root cause of differences in vocabulary, language development, and reading comprehension (Hart and Risley 2003). However, in research from MIT in 2018, scientists led by McGovern Institute investigator John Gabrieli and researcher Rachel Romeo found that increasing conversations between adults and children had a measurable impact on the children's brain growth and cognition. In a study of children ages four to six, the number of back-and-forth conversational turns accounted for differences in brain physiology and language skills, regardless of parental income or education. Their findings indicate that back-and-forth conversation is more critical to language development than the "30 million word gap" (Romeo et al. 2021). A study by Weisleder and Fernald (2013) found that children from low-income families with access to play materials and adult-child interactions promoting language development had more extensive vocabularies and better language skills than children from similar incomes without this access.

Clearly, caregivers can significantly influence children's language and brain development simply by engaging them in conversation. The key is having a two-way dialogue, which can be counterintuitive to many adults' inherent instinct to talk *at* children versus *with* them. This conversational exchange helps develop children's language skills more than just exposing them to large quantities of words. Interestingly, the number of conversational turns strongly predicted children's performance on language assessments including vocabulary, grammar, and reasoning (Romeo et al. 2021).

These findings offer us a glimpse into how critical it is for caregivers to engage young children in conversation. Simple interactions like turn-taking with sounds or facial expressions can make a difference even before speech develops. And even though more conversation typically occurs in families from higher incomes, any child exposed to interactive exchange gains language benefits. Conversational turn-taking influences children's brain development and the growth of their language capacities.

In the race to prepare children for academic success, we've left behind good old basic talking in favor of prereading skills and hitting milestones sooner rather than later. Most of the conversations with adults that children engage in are commands, demands, or instructions. There are few deep conversations during which the child is expressing important feelings and thoughts.

Educators can learn many helpful techniques for engaging in meaningful conversations with the children in their care. I recently picked up the book *The Art of Talking with Children*, in which author Rebecca Rolland (2022) gives several important tips she calls the ABCs of rich talk:

- **Adaptive.** Meaningful conversations require that we adapt to the child we're talking with. Adapting means we're paying attention to their words, tone, and body language cues and adjusting our words and tone in response. I keep a conversation notebook for making notes of what the child talked about, their tone and body cues, and what's working in our conversations.
- **Back and forth.** Engaging in a back-and-forth conversation is the heart of any meaningful verbal communication. It's the dance of the speaking and listening in which connection is made. Demonstrate that you're listening closely by using body cues like nodding and leaning forward, making comments like "Tell me more" and "Yeah," and offering reflective sounds like "hmm." These cues let the child know you're interested and are ready to hear more.
- **Child driven.** Let the child's interests and ideas guide the conversation. Start by bringing up topics or questions you know they want to discuss, since beginning with the child's own perspective immediately makes it meaningful. This approach allows the child to practice sharing their ideas in a safe space. Keeping the conversation child-driven ensures that the child is gaining critical language skills and isn't just a passive participant in the exchange. It also places focus on their interests, skills, and emerging capabilities.

Another tool that helps me have personal conversations with children, especially in a large class, is Julie Starr's 4 Levels of Listening framework (Starr 2023). Use this framework as a check-in so you can thoughtfully answer the question "What kind of listening am I providing right now?" Throughout your day, you'll use all four levels. For personal conversations with individual children, make sure you are listening at a level 3 or 4. (See the Listening Awareness Reflection Form in appendix B on page 160 for a reflective tool to help you use this framework.)

- **Level 1: Cosmetic Listening.** "I look like I'm listening, but I'm not fully with you. I'm thinking about other things right now." This is a passive form of listening where our thoughts are somewhere else. It's also called superficial listening. It's like talking to the clerk at your grocery store—you have no authentic investment in the conversation. It's polite and requires no effort.
- **Level 2: Conversational Listening.** "I'm listening in order to respond. I'm thinking about what I want to say." This is the most common type of listening. It's another passive form of conversation in which you're more invested in what you have to say than listening to the other person.
- **Level 3: Active Listening.** "I'm focused on what you're saying, and you have my full attention." At this level, an important shift happens. You're now listening actively and are focused on what the other person is saying with full intention. You spend more time listening and processing what's being said than speaking. The child will know that you're listening because you're making sounds, gestures, and comments to affirm your attention. Additionally, you might use clarifying questions and paraphrase what the child said to affirm your understanding of what they just said.
- **Level 4: Deep Listening.** "I'm more focused on you than me, I'm getting a sense of who you are right now." You focus completely on the child, their words and meanings. You demonstrate genuine interest that leaves the child feeling seen, heard, and valued.

When we're great listeners of children, we make space for the child to express their views, thoughts, and concerns. Here are more tips:

- Be an attentive presence.
  - » Show your interest by using nonverbal gestures, for example, nods, eye contact, smiles, and even leaning forward.
  - » Don't interrupt.
  - » Give space for silence. Some children need space to form their thoughts.
- Make sure you can hear what is being said and see the child's body language.

- As you listen, try to put yourself in the shoes of the child. Can you see their viewpoint?
- Replay the child's words back to them to communicate that you've been listening carefully.

As we conclude this chapter, and our examination of the fourth pillar of the PAL model, we now have a deeper and more nuanced understanding of the role of children's voices in their learning and development. We can see that there are many vital dimensions to voice, including how it informs the work we do as educators as well as the many ways it supports children's academic learning and development.

We can now also appreciate how vital it is to encourage and uplift children's voices in the learning setting. By doing so, we're helping set a precedent for them that they are capable, competent, and valued, in their own beautiful and brilliant ways. Each pillar of the PAL model is important, and they all support and contribute to one another. In this future-looking context, however, voice not only supports the other pillars but also sets the stage for a lifetime of healthy expression and exploration.

### GOLD NUGGETS

- When children's opinions, thoughts, and ideas are heard and valued, it supports their emerging identity, nurtures their intelligences, and demonstrates respect.
- Engaging children in meaningful, back-and-forth conversations significantly affects their language and brain development.

## THE PRACTICE OF THE EDUCATOR: EXCHANGING

Within this pillar of the PAL model, the educator finds themselves in a unique and wonderful position to engage in the exchange of ideas with children. With an understanding of and respect for the voices of children, this practice offers opportunities for reciprocity and joyful learning for both the child and educator. Put simply, when we view the ways in which children's voices matter, not only in the context of their development but in the ways their voices express their innate brilliance, the exchange of ideas and perspectives becomes an energizing and fun experience for both parties.

> **Aha Note!**
>
> When children's voices are valued—their opinions, feelings, thoughts, and preferences are heard—we support their emerging identity and nurture their innate intelligences.

It's through this exchange of ideas and perspectives that we support children's thinking processes. With a nonjudgmental approach and lack of a predetermined agenda, we encourage children to explore and expand their thinking processes in a safe context. Through our exchange, we're providing a safe space where they can try out new ways of thinking and expression that they can then carry forth into their learning experiences and lives.

The primary ways in which we can facilitate this exchange are through our conversations with children as well as through Learning Stories. Conversations, of course, are an equal exchange of ideas and perspectives, supported by our active listening practices. Learning Stories, a method created by Wendy Lee and Margaret Carr, are narratives crafted from what an educator knows about a child, which can be contributed to by the child and even their families or caregivers. These are stories that highlight what children can do versus what they can't. They provide a view into a child's learning journey, including things like their interests, sense of resourcefulness, and motivation. In this way, a Learning Story is essentially an analysis of a child's learning experience, lovingly written by the educator. It is a far more rewarding exchange of information than the standard status report offered by the assembly line paradigm.

Through the flow of exchange that takes place between child and educator, the stage is set for bolstering their identity as a thriving learner. It is through this practice of exchange that we can further shine a light on and nurture children's wonderful, innate brilliance.

CHAPTER 7

# LEARNER IDENTITY

Teachers who put relationships first don't just have students for one year; they have students who view them as "their" teacher for life.
—Justin Tarte

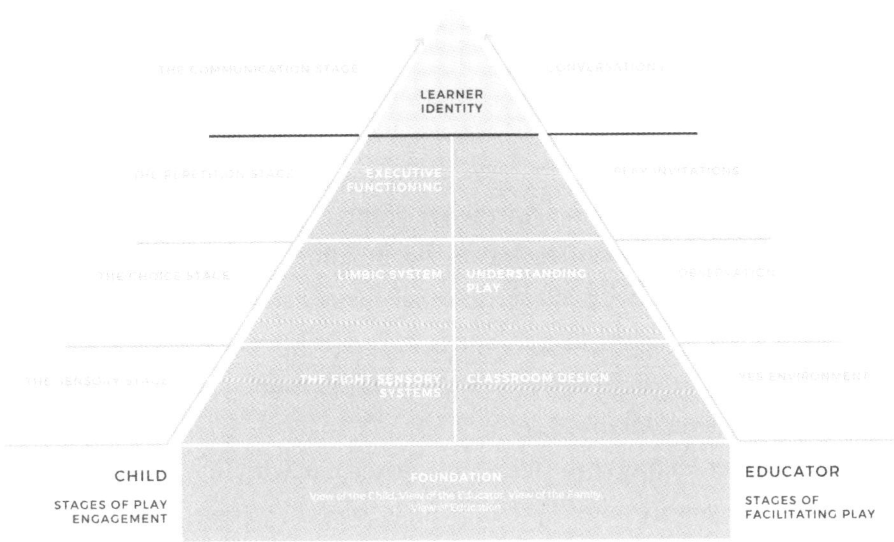


As we reach the culmination of the four pillars of the Play-Activated Learning (PAL) model, we'll explore learner identity and think about how your relationship to the child is more important than any material, activity, or strategy. In the context of how we've approached the previous pillars thus far, note that this chapter functions as an extension of the previous chapter, which covered the Voice stage and the practice of exchange through conversation, by looking more deeply at the capstone piece of the pyramid, learner identity. The intention is to highlight how these pillars come together to contribute to the overall identity of the learner.

My career in education came about because of my own child's struggles. I also struggled in school as a child. What is similar about my son's experience and my own is that we both had educators who were more concerned with achieving the mandated outcomes than supporting the child standing in front of them.

It blows my mind that we are *still* fighting to do what's right in the early childhood setting. Alfie Kohn wrote in his 1999 book *Punished by Rewards: The Trouble with Gold Stars, Incentive Plans, A's, Praise, and Other Bribes*, "If children feel safe, they can take risks, ask questions, make mistakes, learn to trust, share their feelings, and grow" (255). A child will feel safe when they know the educator genuinely cares about their needs and feelings.

A child's connection with the educator is the foundation of the learning environment. It is the beginning of their identity as a learner. Supporting and facilitating the development of the child's sense of identity as a learner is the most powerful way to prepare them for academic learning—and encourage the further unfolding of their innate brilliance.

I became very interested in the learner identity in my setting when I was teaching at Head Start. In my first year as the lead teacher, I had a student who had been in thirteen foster homes by the age of three. His defense mechanism was biting other children when he felt threatened. Building a relationship of trust and safety was clearly my priority. I kept a journal of my relationship with Mickey and his struggles. His biting was instant and fast, and it was as if it was the only way he had to protect himself. Unfortunately, his swift movement of protection often landed on the other children's cheeks.

Every day I met Mickey at the door and greeted him with "I've been waiting for you. I'm so happy you are here." I wanted him to know he was welcome and important to me. At first, he wouldn't even look at me. He played by himself, watching the other children. Every day, I gave Mickey verbal and nonverbal communications that he was important to me. I stayed the course and hoped for the best.

Several months into the year, Mickey stopped biting. It went as suddenly as it had arrived. One huge milestone was that he was being adopted by a wonderful couple and his new moms were extraordinary in their support and love. Mickey was thriving at home, and he was thriving at school. His learner identity began to emerge and blossom. He needed safety and trust at home, and he needed safety and trust at school to become a highly engaged learner and thrive as a child.

Working with Mickey fascinated me. He couldn't connect to me or the community until he felt safe and seen. I developed the following model to make sense of what I was noticing:

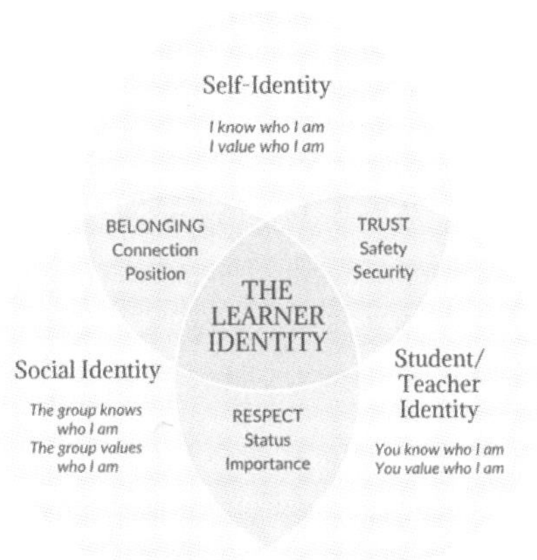


My learner identity model has three primary dimensions:

- How the child perceives themselves as a learner, their **self-identity**
- How the child believes the teacher perceives them as a learner, the **student/teacher identity**
- How the child thinks the community perceives them as a learner, the **social identity**

## SELF-IDENTITY: THE CHILD'S RELATIONSHIP TO THEIR SELF

Before we consider children's self-identity from a developmental perspective, we, as adults and educators, must adjust our lens to be sure we are viewing each child as an amazing, capable communicator of their own ideas, feelings, and views. Put simply, children are the best, most informed communicators of their self-identity. It is our task to trust and respect their capability in this communication. As educators, we can observe children's sense of "I know who I am" through their self-expression and self-awareness. And we see their sense of "I value who I am" through their self-esteem and self-confidence. By grounding our understanding of the child's sense of self in these observations, we form a deeper, more meaningful context for our relationship with them.

In a developmental context, self-identity emerges out of a specific kind of memory, known as *episodic memory*. Episodic memory enables a person to recall everyday events and to recount those experiences. Children start to gather information about themselves and store autobiographical material, starting a life narrative that guides their responses to the world.

During early childhood, children start to develop a self-concept. From eighteen to thirty months, children developed their *categorical self*. This is a concrete way of viewing themselves in "this or that" labels. For example, young children label themselves in terms of age, "child or adult"; physical characteristics, "short or tall"; and value, "good or bad." These labels that children use to describe their self-concept are very concrete, observable terms. For example, a child may describe himself this way: "I'm four. I have blue eyes. I'm shorter than Mommy. I can help Grandma set the table!"

Within the context of the learner identity model, children with a developed learning identity view themselves as capable, competent learners. They seek and engage in life experiences with a more open-minded, growth-oriented approach and believe, at a deep and instinctual level, in their ability to learn. The learning identity is strongly influenced by their important relationships, including those with their educators and peers.

At the juncture of the child's self-identity and the student-educator identity is trust. Children will feel safe and trust the environment when they feel their teacher not only likes them but values who they are as an individual.

Safety for young children means there are no perceived threats from the teacher. A perceived threat includes a sense of the educator's attachment—or lack of attachment—to the child. As our brain is wired to keep us alive, it's constantly scanning the environment for anything that might be perceived as a threat or reward. When we consider this from the viewpoint of a child and their perception of their relationship with their educator, we can appreciate the deep need for trust. Trust absolutely must be present to fully support and nurture the learner identity.

## STUDENT-TEACHER IDENTITY: THE CHILD'S RELATIONSHIP TO THE EDUCATOR

Children gather information about who they are in the context of the people around them, and this information builds their narrative about who they are. Their first context in this sense is, of course, their parents and family. As they enter the learning environment, their relationship with their educators also becomes an important and integral part of this information gathering. While the nature of the relationship is different from that of parents and family, it is significant and vital to the development of their identities as learners and valued human beings.

Considering this dimension from the child's perspective, their sense of "You know who I am" is indicated by their attachment and sense of status (their perception of how they're regarded) with their educator. The child's sense of "You value who I am" is expressed through their feelings of security and trust for the educator.

If the educator doesn't feel connected to the child (or worse, doesn't like the child), then trust, safety, and security can't exist. This is not science—it's common sense. Think about the last time you gathered with a few friends and were approached by someone whom one of you didn't like. It immediately changes the conversational climate. Safety and trust in the learning environment begins with the child's relationship to the educator.

In the assembly line model of education, a child has no voice and no choice. The dynamic is teacher driven, with compliance at the heart of the system. Inside this model, the educator approaches each child with the same curriculum and outcomes. The educator builds a relationship to the child based on academic outcomes and achievements through testing and assessments, versus fostering a relationship *with* the child.

When we bring honor and reverence to each child and their personal learning journey, it builds the foundation for a strong learner identity. Our primary task is to find a connection with each child (see appendix B for Practices of Connection on page 161). In so doing, we are nurturing a dynamic in which they can thrive, both academically and personally. In our efforts to foster this connection, we may ask ourselves these questions:

- What do you appreciate about each child?
- What do you enjoy about each child?

If I find I'm not connecting with a child, I take time to talk to them and really get to know them. When a child has a powerful relationship of "belonging" to the teacher, they will have status and importance in the setting.

An article from the Center on the Developing Child at Harvard University states the following: "Healthy brain architecture depends on a sturdy foundation built by appropriate input from a child's senses and stable, responsive relationships with caring adults. If an adult's responses to a child are unreliable, inappropriate, or simply absent, the developing architecture of the brain may be disrupted, and subsequent physical, mental, and emotional health may be impaired." Responsive educators are pivotal contributors to a thriving architecture and flourishing learner identity.

At the juncture of the student-teacher identity and the social identity is respect. As these two dimensions intersect and affect one another, the child will feel seen, heard, and valued as a full member of the classroom. They will have a sense of importance to the teacher and to the larger group. Giving your attention to each child and responding with positive intent (that is, positively contributing to their student-teacher identity) is critical for children to feel a sense of honor and respect in the context of their social identity.

The feeling of not being respected triggers the limbic brain centers, where our instincts drive our behaviors, and results in a sense of being unsafe. For example, when a child is interrupted when speaking or their ideas are not considered, the instinctual part of their brain, sometimes called the reptilian brain, is triggered. This is the part of the brain that not only controls the most basic autonomic bodily functions—like breathing—but also responds to perceived threats, both physical and verbal.

When we consider respect in this context, we can appreciate that it's much more than a "valuable dynamic" in the classroom. It's at the core of prosocial functioning and sets the stage for a fruitful learner identity at a deeply ingrained level.

## SOCIAL IDENTITY: THE CHILD'S RELATIONSHIP TO COMMUNITY

As educators, we are in a unique position to encourage and assist in the development of the third aspect of this model, children's social identity. How you view a child affects how the child's peers in the setting view them, which will, in turn, influence their identity. The social identity is the starting point of every community, as the individual's sense of their place and value within the group contributes to the collective nature of the group.

Children build secure and strong relationships with one another in the classroom. By gathering information from these relationships about who they are and how they're regarded by their peers, their social identity is further developed and becomes a foundation of their learner identity. From the child's perspective, a sense of "The group knows who I am" is cultivated as they feel recognition and respect from the group. A sense of "The group values who I am" comes as they feel belonging and appreciation.

Social relationships provide a structure for children to learn essential social skills. Thus far we've been looking at the vertical relationship of child to educator. Now we'll consider the horizontal relationships between peers. Both help children acquire social knowledge vital to their future relationships and general well-being in the world.

The respect and status of the child inside the community affects the child's self-identity as a learner. For example, children who have behavioral challenges are often shamed because they're not capable of complying. I've seen educators put rewards and punishments in place for the entire classroom community because of one or two children's behavior. This only serves to further shame the struggling child and creates social isolation.

When children have conflicts in our environments, as the educator, we should not take over the conflict as the "expert of resolution" or dominate it. Resolution is a mighty endeavor at the heart of the early childhood setting. It is our work. We don't lament, "Oh, no, they're fighting all the time." No, they're learning what it means to coexist with other human beings. How many adults have great conflict resolution skills? In truth, not many, because no one took the time to teach us. When we take the time to have each child within a conflict speak their truth, it communicates to all children that their viewpoints are important. They each hold a position of respect in our setting.

Traditionally, the position of power and respect is automatically given to the teacher, and children hold no position of power. In child-led education, every child in the community walks in with equal position; they don't have to earn a position of respect. You're given respect and power the moment you walk into the room. Every child holds this position, even if they struggle behaviorally.

As the social identity and the self-identity of the child come together, a sense of belonging is established and nurtured. Children will feel belonging and a sense of position in the classroom when they perceive their contribution to the group as valued individuals.

As we discussed previously, the child's brain is constantly scanning the physical environment for possible threats. The child is also closely monitoring the social environment—whether or not the child is interacting with others. More specifically, regardless of whether the child is playing in a center, running around outside, or listening to a story, they are closely scrutinizing others' behavior at a deep, limbic level. Any perceived threat can trigger the fight, flight, or freeze response in the brain. When one of these responses is activated, children resist or won't take on new challenges, won't ask questions or speak up in class conversations, and avoid all sorts of risks. In other words, the child will not be fully self-expressed as their authentic selves and tap into their full potential.

## NURTURING A LIFETIME OF LEARNING

With the four pillars of the PAL model as our foundation, in this chapter we've looked at how children view themselves in the context of their self-beliefs. We've also explored their beliefs about how educators and their communities view them, and in all three contexts, how these beliefs contribute to their identities as learners. We're now equipped to do our utmost as educators to nurture each child's robust and thriving learner identity. This identity not only fosters growth and development in the immediate sense but also paves the way for a lifetime of approaching new learning opportunities with an attitude of openness and even adventure. In essence, by setting the stage for early wonder, agency, and exploration, we're cultivating a mindset of growth and self-confidence that will carry into all aspects of life and into adulthood.

As educators, our role is based very much in the here and now and the many opportunities throughout our day to encourage and nurture the growth mindset. As we come to understand the implications of those here-and-now moments, however, we can begin to have a deeper understanding and regard for the foundation we're helping create with the children in our care. We won't always (and often, never) see the outcome of our efforts in the far future, and we are rarely privy to the full unfolding of children's brilliance as they develop into young adults and thriving human beings. We can, however, embrace our work wholeheartedly and with full confidence that *the work we do matters*. We are providing children, to the best of our ability, with every opportunity to step into their lives with a love of learning—one that can potentially take them anywhere they want to go in the future.

## GOLD NUGGETS

- The relationship between the teacher and the child is more important than any material, activity, or strategy.
- A child's connection with the educator is the foundation of the learning environment and the beginning of their identity as a learner.
- Educators play a vital role in influencing how children are perceived by their peers, which, in turn, affects the child's social identity and sense of belonging in the group.

## THE PRACTICE OF EDUCATOR: THE LEARNER IDENTITY

I wanted to highlight the lack of value that worksheets bring to young children and the development of the learner identity and nurturing a child's brilliance.

Consider the worksheet below:

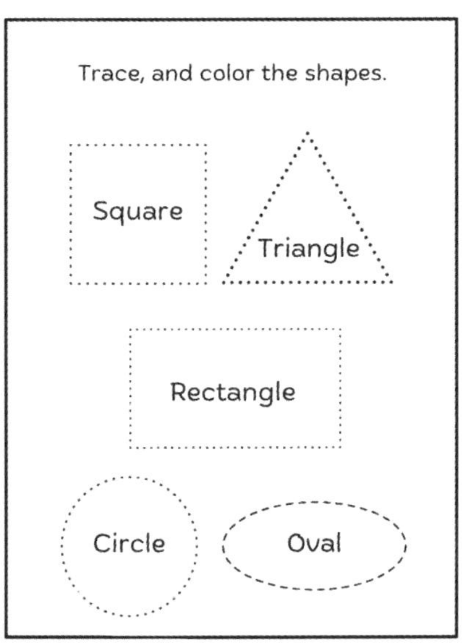


*Aha Note!*

Safety and trust in the learning environment begins with the child's relationship to the educator.

Viewing this worksheet through the lens of the learner identity model, now consider the following:

- **Self-Identity:** Children gather and internalize information about who they are in the context of activities given to them. What information is a child discovering about themselves in a worksheet like this one? How does this worksheet support children in finding self-value?
- **Student-Educator Identity:** Children gather and internalize information about who they are in the context of the people around them—this builds their narrative about who they are. How does tracing these shapes support a child building attachment to the educator? How does this support a child feeling valued by their teacher?
- **Social Identity:** Children gather and internalize information about who they are in the context of their peers. This builds their narrative about who they are and their value in the world. How does this worksheet help a child discover who they are with their peers? How does it build a sense of belonging? How does it help a child feel valued by their peers?

We can hopefully see from this illustration the need to very intentionally break away from things like cookie-cutter art in which all projects look the same. In these kinds of teacher-directed activities, the child's thinking is passive. There is no choice or decision-making, as the outcome has already been decided with little to no room for the learner identity to develop. While these kinds of activities have been the longtime standard of the assembly line paradigm, we now understand how deeply counter to children's developmental processes and needs they are.

As play-based educators, we can do better.

CHAPTER 8

# Harnessing the Innate Intelligences of the Whole Child

Play isn't a precursor to "real" learning; it is a method of evolving that facilitates higher intelligence.
—Nathan Wallis

| PILLAR | DOMAIN | INTELLIGENCE |
|---|---|---|
| Permission | Physical Self | Self-Regulation |
| Choice | Social/Emotional Self | Self-Awareness |
| Repetition | Cognitive Self | Self-Perseverance |
| Voice | Embodied Self | Self-Expression |

When children are given access to free play, a miraculous thing happens. Hidden in the fabric of play are the mechanics of developing the whole child—the physical, social/emotional, cognitive, and spiritual (which I am calling embodied) self. And underlying the Play-Activated Learning (PAL) model are four intelligences embedded within its pillars—self-regulation, self-awareness, self-perseverance, and self-expression. (Find Harnessing the Innate Intelligences of the Whole Child in appendix B on page 162.) These intelligences are supported and nurtured by each of the four pillars and play a crucial role in children's blossoming into whole, thriving human beings.

In the late 1970s, Howard Gardner developed a theory of multiple intelligences. Gardner asserted there were eight intelligences but that only two were valued in the school system. Gardner argued that intelligence didn't have anything to do with an IQ test but rather, intelligence was "bio-psychological potential to process information that can be activated in a cultural setting to solve problems or create products that are of value in a culture" (Davis et al. 2011). I value his work and feel it holds an important shift in perspective. I want to be clear, though, that I am not using the same definition of intelligence as Gardner.

I am using the term *intelligence* more in line with the definition of *innate intelligence*. This is not about learning something external to self. Rather, it is the awakening of one's inborn wisdom. It is knowledge gained through experience in life.

Recently, while in the Rocky Mountains, I noticed that the huge dandelions close up their petals when the afternoon rains roll in and then open again when the rains stop. This is innate wisdom. It's unconscious and, given the right circumstances, it naturally arises.

In my years of working with children, I witnessed their innate intelligences of self as they were awakening in their play. Play is the rich soil that nurtures these intelligences. It concerns me deeply that play is disappearing from early childhood classrooms and academic work is widely becoming the priority. "Preparation" for school is killing children's ability to develop these crucial innate intelligences of selfhood.

## THE INTELLIGENCE OF THE PHYSICAL SELF: SELF-REGULATION

Over my years in the classroom, I witnessed firsthand how children develop distinct intelligences through play. The first class I taught in Head Start as a lead educator (three-year-olds) is a prime example. The first day of class, the children were literally jumping off tables and running wild. Developing self-regulation was going to be front and center. My Waldorf training had talked about setting up obstacle courses where the children could walk a balance beam, jump over sticks, crawl through a tunnel, and more. I set up an indoor obstacle course. The children loved it and would do it again and again. I would often change it or add to it to keep the novelty alive. This class spent months obsessed with that obstacle course.

By honoring the physical needs of the children, the innate intelligence of self-regulation emerged and the children gained mastery over their own bodies. Their ability to control their emotional responses increased too. Studies have shown that "the more time children spend in unstructured quiet play in the toddler and preschool years, the better their self-regulation abilities at ages 4–5 and 6–7 years" (Colliver et al. 2022). When you give permission, a yes environment, for children to get their physical needs met, you are providing rich opportunities for the development of intelligence such as self-regulation.

## THE INTELLIGENCE OF THE SOCIAL/ EMOTIONAL SELF: SELF-AWARENESS

When we offer children free play, we are giving them free choice, as discussed in chapter 4. Imagine a child making choices every day during play and developing a sense of what is satisfying in their chosen activities. Over time this builds their sense of what their interests, preferences, and needs are in play. An awareness of self arises, and the social/emotional self is fortified.

Maggie, a three-year-old attending forest school, played in the large sand area under a huge magnolia tree nearly every day. At the beginning of school, I noticed how she would immediately go to the sand pile. She would wander around the pile, digging up sand and dumping it, and picking up fallen magnolia leaves and scooping with them in the sand.

After a few months, she started wandering the yard. She would visit the chickens, ride a bike, and sit on stumps. Slowly, she became fascinated with the chickens. She would help feed the chickens in their coop. Then she would carry them around. She noticed details about each chicken. Interestingly, she even had a preferred way of carrying the chickens and would sing as she fed them. By Maggie being allowed the space and freedom to discover what *her* interests were, she connected to something that captured her heart—the care and feeding of chickens. Maggie became aware of something she cared about deeply and how she desired to go about it. This is the emerging intelligence of self-awareness.

## THE INTELLIGENCE OF THE COGNITIVE SELF: SELF-PERSEVERANCE

In chapter 5, we took a look at the power of repetition in play. It is through repetition that a remarkable intelligence is awakened—self-perseverance. I remember Charlie, a four-year old, who was determined to walk the long balance beam on the playground. Every day he would run to the balance beam and try to walk on it. He could take a few steps but would fall.

One day I noticed Charlie watching his friends walk the balance beam. He sat for quite a while before getting up and trying yet again. His arms went out and he moved slowly, one foot at a time. This time he made it halfway! Charlie was overjoyed.

"Mrs. Haughey, tomorrow I am going to walk the whole thing. Just wait!" he shouted as we went back inside.

The next day Charlie begged me to watch him as he was certain he was going to conquer the balance beam. Slowly he stepped onto the beam. Out went his arms as he carefully placed one foot in front of the other. When he began to lose his balance, he used his arms to steady himself. Finally, he made it to the end of the beam. His eyes were bright with accomplishment.

"Watch me do it again!" And sure enough, he did it again.

Charlie had figured out how to master the balance beam through the innate intelligence of not only his body but from his observation of others who could do it. This self-perseverance that he gained through walking the beam penetrated every aspect of his learner identity. It was like Charlie had emerged from a cocoon.

Play provides opportunities for young children to harness their desire for mastery, and in doing so, it awakens their perseverance to achieve it. This builds the foundation of cognitive development. Today's typical early childhood settings do not provide the opportunity for young children to repeatedly attempt to master desired abilities and develop one of the most important life skills—perseverance.

## THE INTELLIGENCE OF THE EMBODIED SELF: SELF-EXPRESSION

One year Olivia, a kindergartener, told me a story about a family of fairies. At the time I was practicing "story plays"—a technique of storytelling inspired by Vivian

Paley. In short, a child would tell me a story and we would act it out. Olivia's first story play was about a family of fairies who loved to drink orange juice and play in the trees.

Olivia loved the story of the fairies so much, she asked to write a book about the Fairy Family. Next, she wanted to paint the fairies. What followed was magic. Her paintings of the fairies became very distinct. Father Fairy had blue and yellow stripes. Mother Fairy was purple with pink dots. Lottie Fairy was pink with tiny flowers. Baby Fairy was pale blue with purple dots. Olivia began adding more and more details to the Fairies. Her personality and unique perspectives were emerging as she unleashed her innate intelligence of self-expression. This is the embodied self. Play is such an incredible cultivator of personal self-expression.

## BRINGING IT ALL TOGETHER

It is my hope that this book makes visible the urgent need for play-based education. I believe play is the rich soil for the potential of young children. I think of it like this: If you toss a handful of wildflower seeds into good dirt, you can watch the natural and incredible blooming of each flower. Each has its own unique unfolding, its own wonderful innate brilliance.

When we take play away, we're stealing the discovery that occurs in play and hindering the development of self. Play is nature's way of developing a young human being. Not worksheets. Not tablet games. And certainly not a one-size-fits-all approach to learning.

With a foundation of clarity about our views of the child and our roles as early childhood educators, we've just taken quite a journey together through the four pillars of the PAL model.

As I sit and ponder how to conclude our time, I'm struck by two things. First, my hope for you, reader, is that within the academic nature of the material we've just covered, you've found a foundation of understanding that you can carry forth into your practice and into your conversations with families, administrators, and peers. I know these conversations can be one of the most challenging aspects of our work. Thank you for arming yourself with this information and fighting the good fight to serve and nurture children's brilliance in ways that honor and respect them.

This brings me to my second thought for you. As I mentioned in the early pages of this book, I'm not here to give you a "you must do this" approach. I can't (and won't) give a formula for success in your classroom setting *every single time*, without fail. Human beings just don't work that way—there *is* no cookie-cutter approach. And, because you're here, I don't think that method would resonate with you anyway.

You're here because you have some inkling, perhaps small, perhaps great, that there *is* a better, healthier, more meaningful, and developmentally appropriate way to work with children—one that far outshines the paradigm that traditional classroom settings offer. Trust your instinct here, my friend. It's one of the greatest gifts we have. I want to encourage you to take that instinct, that drive to serve and respect children through your practice, use the information in this book to give it fuel and a framework—and then go influence as many children's lives as you can with it. You already have within you a sense of the wonder and beauty of childhood and know that it deserves a place in education. You may already be practicing within the context of many, most, or even all of the concepts within this book. *But now you have a framework*. You have a way to meet instinct with science, put your stake in the ground, and stand firm in what you believe is best and right for the children in your care.

Thank you for taking this journey with me. In doing so, we've joined together in what I consider one of the most precious and powerful missions—to nurture the blossoming and thriving of children's learning and development, the unfolding of their true brilliance, with the utmost intention and respect for them.

> *Aha Note!*
>
> **Children's innate intelligence of self awakens in their play. Play is the rich soil that nurtures this intelligence.**

## GOLD NUGGETS

- Free play allows children to discover their interests and develop self-awareness and emotional intelligence by exploring their preferences and needs.
- Play is essential for the natural and holistic development of children. It enables them to discover and develop their sense of self, a process that cannot be replicated through structured activities like worksheets or digital games.
- The shift in early childhood education toward academics and away from play is hindering the development of these crucial innate intelligences, potentially affecting children's ability to blossom into whole, thriving individuals.

## THE PRACTICE OF THE EDUCATOR

Morning Pages is a technique introduced by Julia Cameron (2016) in *The Artist's Way: A Spiritual Path to Higher Creativity* designed to cultivate creativity and clarity. This practice has given me the ability to be the educator I wanted to be by clearing the stress and worry. Here's how:

1. Set five to ten minutes each morning to write three pages of longhand, stream-of-consciousness writing. Use a basic spiral notebook.
2. Let your thoughts flow freely onto the page. Don't censor yourself. Put down whatever is in your mind. Let your anger out. Let out the stress and worry. Let out the joy—whatever is there.
3. Don't worry about making sense or sounding good. Don't worry about grammar. No one is going to read this besides you.

Educating can be emotionally demanding. Use Morning Pages to process feelings, frustrations, and joys, helping to prevent burnout and maintain emotional well-being. Morning Pages will often surprise you! My best ideas happened during my Morning Pages. Finally, Morning Pages are for your eyes only. This privacy is crucial for your mind to fully release thoughts with honesty and vulnerability.

Appendix A

# READER'S GUIDE

Below you'll find reflection and discussion and questions and action steps for each chapter in this book as well as applications for your teaching setting. I hope these questions and suggestions help you take the material deeper, provide discussion prompts for your team, and inspire you to strengthen and renew your commitment to trusting play.

## CHAPTER 1: WHAT IS PLAY-ACTIVATED LEARNING?

### Prereading Reflections

1. What motivated you to pick up this book, and what do you hope to learn?
2. Think back on your childhood experiences. How have they influenced your views on education and your role as a teacher?
3. How do you view the role of play in early childhood learning? What experiences or observations have influenced your stand on play-based education?

## CHAPTER 2: THE FOUNDATION

### Personal Reflection

1. What do you believe about teaching and learning? Why educate?
2. What beliefs do you hold around what your role is? What is your image of children?

### Setting Application

1. Examine the routines in your classroom. Where do you see aspects that inadvertently mirror elements of the assembly line model of education? What adjustments could you introduce to create a more child-centered, play-based learning environment?
2. Do you see any traces of old strategies that indirectly shame children? Do you see strategies that promote competition?
3. In what ways could you support families in understanding and respecting individual differences in children's growth and development?

## CHAPTER 3: PERMISSION

### Tactile System

1. Recall a moment when a thoughtful touch brought you comfort and a sense of security. What was it about that touch that made you feel so reassured?
2. How can you use touch to create a sense of welcome and belonging in your setting?
3. Reflect on your environment. What adjustments could you make to offer an array of tactile experiences and sensory experiences?

### Proprioception System

1. Think about activities you enjoy that involve proprioceptive input. How do these activities make you feel?
2. How can you create a classroom environment that provides opportunities for movement throughout the day?
3. Reflect on this statement from my mentor, "The sense of movement is the mother of joy." How have you observed this connection between movement and emotional well-being in children?

## Vestibular System

1. How comfortable are you with activities like spinning, swinging, or being upside down? Do you enjoy or avoid these sensations?
2. What specific activities can you incorporate into your daily schedule to support vestibular development, addressing both linear and rotary movement?
3. Discuss the connection between the vestibular system and the development of skills like reading and writing. How can this understanding guide your expectations and practices in the classroom?

## Olfactory System

1. Think about a scent that evokes a strong memory for you. Describe the scent and the memory it brings back. How does it make you feel?
2. The book suggests that the olfactory system is deeply connected to memory and emotion. How does this understanding influence your approach to teaching and creating memorable learning experiences?
3. Evaluate the current scents present in your classroom environment. What changes can you make to minimize artificial smells and introduce more natural, pleasant scents?

## Gustatory System

1. Think about a memorable meal. What flavors stood out to you, and how did they make you feel?
2. How can you create a positive and nurturing environment for children to explore and develop their gustatory senses, considering their individual preferences and needs?
3. Reflect on the idea, "Our relationship to food touches a very deep place in our sense of trust and security." How does this perspective inform your approach to mealtime routines and your interactions with children around food?

## Interoception System

1. How do you recognize and respond to your own body's signals for hunger, thirst, and fatigue? Have you always been attuned to these signals, or have you learned this over time?
2. What are some specific ways you can help children tune into and understand their body's signals related to hunger, thirst, fatigue, and the need for movement?

## Auditory System

1. How aware are you of the sounds in your environment? Do you find yourself tuning out certain sounds or seeking out others?
2. Consider the idea that live human voices have a distinct impact on the larynx compared to recorded voices. How might you reduce the use of recorded and/or electronic voices (singing with videos from the internet is an example) with children in your care?
3. Review the auditory environment in your classroom. What changes might you implement to reduce noise levels and create a more supportive auditory space?

## Visual System

1. Think about a time when you felt overwhelmed by visual clutter. How did it affect your mood?
2. How does the concept of "visual noise" challenge traditional notions of classroom design and decoration?
3. Reflect on your learning environment. What elements might contribute to visual noise or distraction? How can you reduce visual clutter to create a more calming atmosphere?

## CHAPTER 4: CHOICE

### Personal Reflection

1. Think back to your childhood. Remember the times when you were given the freedom to make choices while playing and learning. How did those moments affect your growth and development?
2. How comfortable are you with letting go of control and allowing children to make their own choices, even if those choices lead to unexpected outcomes?
3. What are your beliefs about the role of the educator in a play-based learning environment? How do your beliefs guide your capacity in giving children choices?

### Setting Application

1. Name some way that you can balance the need for structure and safety with providing children with more freedom to choose.
2. Audit your classroom to identify areas where children's choices are limited. What changes can you make to increase their autonomy?

## CHAPTER 5: REPETITION

### Personal Reflection

1. Have you ever felt stressed or anxious due to a lack of structure or predictability in your routine? How did this situation affect your perception of the significance of having a routine?
2. Consider a task or talent that you have perfected by practicing it. How did the act of practicing this task aid in your learning and personal development?
3. Recall a time when you observed a child repeating the same activity daily. How did this repetition influence the child's engagement and development?

### Setting Application

1. Observe children's patterns of play (schemas) over the course of a week. What activities do they gravitate toward repeatedly? How can you build on these interests to deepen their learning and engagement?
2. In what ways does repetition build sustained focus and attention, and how does this support the development of executive functioning?
3. How can understanding children's play urges through repetition inform your use of invitations, provocations, and inquiries?

## CHAPTER 6: VOICE

### Personal Reflection

1. Reflect on your own experiences as a child. How were your communicated ideas and interests respected and valued by the adults in your life? Were the things you cared about appreciated?
2. How safe was it to speak your mind?
3. How did this affect your sense of self and ability to express yourself?

### Setting Application

1. How can you incorporate children's ideas, interests, and theories into your planning in a way that empowers them as active participants in their learning?
2. How can you ensure that quieter or less vocal children have opportunities to express themselves and be heard?
3. Knowing that conversations play a crucial role in expanding children's vocabulary and building literacy skills, what might be next steps?

## CHAPTER 7: LEARNER IDENTITY

### Personal Reflection

1. Did you ever feel "seen and valued" by one of your teachers? What was the impact of being seen?
2. Do you remember a teacher or teachers with whom you felt invisible or for whom you felt you could never be enough? What was the impact of that?

### Setting Application

1. Trust is a crucial intersection between a child's self-identity and their relationship with the educator. How do you establish and maintain trust with the children in your care? What are your daily, weekly, and monthly strategies?
2. How can your perception of a child affect their social identity within the classroom? What strategies do you use to ensure that each child feels valued and competent in your room?

## CHAPTER 8: HARNESSING THE INNATE INTELLIGENCES OF THE WHOLE CHILD

### Personal Reflection

1. In what ways could you integrate the concept of innate intelligence into your teaching practice to support the children's development?
2. Reflect on a time when you observed a child's innate intelligence emerging through play. How did it affect your understanding of their development?

## Setting Application

1. Observe the children's free play closely. What evidence do you see of the four intelligences emerging in their interactions, choices, and activities? Document specific examples for each intelligence (self-regulation, self-awareness, self-perseverance, and self-expression). What do you see that supports the growth and development of the intelligences?
2. How might you engage families in understanding the value of play in developing these four intelligences? Think about strategies to communicate the importance of play and how families can support their children's play at home.

Appendix B

# Observation, Reflection, and Planning Forms

## CHAPTER 2: OBSERVATION OF THE STATEMENTS YOU USE WITH CHILDREN

**Exercise:** Record yourself in the classroom in thirty-minute segments. Afterward, listen to the recording and check off all the different types of statements you hear yourself use. Use one check mark per statement (for example, if you gave five commanding statements, mark off five boxes).

| TYPE OF STATEMENT | | | | | | | |
|---|---|---|---|---|---|---|---|
| **Commanding/Directing:** *"Sit tall." "Walk quietly."* | | | | | | | |
| **Punishing/Threatening:** *"If you act like this, then you will not be able to play here anymore today."* | | | | | | | |
| **Discounting/Dismissing:** *"I am not too sure that is the truth; we will have to look further."* | | | | | | | |
| **Shaming/Belittling:** *"I have told you a hundred times, don't put the paint in dramatic play. What am I going to do with you?"* | | | | | | | |
| **Informational/ Explanatory:** *"Today we are baking bread."* | | | | | | | |
| **Questioning/Inquiring:** *"What do you think will happen if we mix these colors?"* | | | | | | | |
| **Validating/Affirming:** *"You're feeling really sad right now, and that's okay."* | | | | | | | |

# CHAPTER 3: REVIEW OF THE SENSES IN THE ENVIRONMENT

| SENSE | CHECKLIST ITEM | YES ✓ | PARTIAL – | NO X | NOTES AND IDEAS |
|---|---|---|---|---|---|
| **Tactile System** | A wide variety of tactile materials are available for exploration. | | | | |
| | Soft, calming textures are available for self-soothing. | | | | |
| | Sensory bins or stations are available for calming breaks. | | | | |
| **Propriocep-tive System** | Activities include opportu-nities for heavy work (e.g., pushing, pulling). | | | | |
| | Seating and positioning options support physical comfort and awareness. | | | | |
| | Spaces for heavy work activi-ties (like pushing/pulling) are provided. | | | | |
| **Vestibular System** | Movement activities (e.g., rocking, balancing) are safe and engaging. | | | | |
| | Tools like wobble stools or balance beams are available. | | | | |
| **Olfactory System** | Classroom smells are neutral or calming, not distracting. | | | | |
| | Environment is free from strong or overwhelming odors. | | | | |
| | Air quality is monitored and supportive of all children. | | | | |

| SENSE | CHECKLIST ITEM | YES ✓ | PARTIAL – | NO X | NOTES AND IDEAS |
|---|---|---|---|---|---|
| **Gustatory System** | Food-related activities respect dietary needs and preferences. | | | | |
| **Interoceptive System** | Children have regular opportunities to check in with their bodies (e.g., hydration, bathroom needs). | | | | |
| | Mindfulness or self-regulation tools are accessible. | | | | |
| **Auditory System** | Opportunities for auditory exploration are available, such as during music or sound play activities. | | | | |
| | Environment is free from loud or overwhelming sounds. | | | | |
| | Educator's voice tone and pace promote comfort and connection. | | | | |
| **Visual System** | Environment is free from visual clutter or overwhelming stimuli | | | | |
| | Visual displays reflect children's interests and foster belonging. | | | | |
| | Areas for visual rest (e.g., blank walls, soft colors) are available. | | | | |

## CHAPTER 4: FOLLOW THE VERB CHECKLIST

Child's Name:

Put a check by the verbs you see in action. Add verbs you witness that are not listed.

| | | | | | |
|---|---|---|---|---|---|
| attaching | | gathering | | racing | |
| balancing | | grabbing | | rolling | |
| bridging | | heightening | | rowing | |
| capturing | | hitching on | | running | |
| carrying | | holding | | shoving | |
| collecting | | hooking up | | sorting | |
| crossing | | joining up | | spilling | |
| dropping | | lining up | | spinning | |
| dumping | | linking | | stacking | |
| enclosing | | moving | | tossing | |
| expanding | | ordering | | transferring | |
| extending | | placing | | trapping | |
| fasten | | piling | | | |
| flying | | pushing | | | |

# CHAPTER 4: DEVELOPMENTAL STAGES OF BLOCK PLAY

Child's Name:

Date:

### *Stage 1: Tote & Carry*

Description:

- Carries blocks around or piles them
- Engages in a full sensory experience (smoothness, weight, size, sounds)

Observed: ☐ Yes ☐ No
Notes:

### *Stage 2: Building Begins*

Description:

- Piles blocks to create a tower
- Lays blocks in rows, either horizontally or vertically
- Demonstrates repetition in building
- Begins to use imagination with props (e.g., cars or trucks on "roads")

Observed: ☐ Yes ☐ No
Notes:

### *Stage 3: Bridging*

Description:

- Experiments with connecting two blocks with a space in between using a third block
- Learns through trial and error, exploring balance and developing eye-hand coordination

Observed: ☐ Yes ☐ No
Notes:

### *Stage 4: Enclosures*

Description:

- Creates enclosed spaces with blocks.
- Demonstrates understanding of inside and outside.
- Engages in the first technical acts of block building.
- Uses props more intentionally to enhance the building process.

Observed: ☐ Yes ☐ No
Notes:

### *Stage 5: Representational Building*

Description:

- Utilizes symmetry, patterns, balance, and designs in constructions
- Names structures and announces their functions
- Incorporates elements of dramatic play into block building

Observed: ☐ Yes ☐ No
Notes:

### *Stage 6: Complex Building*

Description:

- Constructs curved buildings and multiple levels
- Builds over other structures and incorporates various materials

Observed: ☐ Yes ☐ No
Notes:

**Special Note:** The stages of block play were first developed by Elizabeth Hirsch in *The Block Book*, first edition 1976. It is still a must-read book.

# CHAPTER 4: DEVELOPMENTAL STAGES OF LOOSE PARTS PLAY

| STAGE | DESCRIPTION | OBSERVED | NOTES |
|---|---|---|---|
| **Stage 1: Transportation & Pile** | • Loose parts are transported, dumped, and scattered. | ☐ Yes ☐ No | |
| | • Little to no symbolic use of loose parts. | ☐ Yes ☐ No | |
| **Stage 2: Shape & Form** | • Child begins to gather and dwell with the loose parts. | ☐ Yes ☐ No | |
| | • Simple forms and first representational use of loose parts emerge. | ☐ Yes ☐ No | |
| **Stage 3: Schematic** | • Full imaginative use of loose parts. | ☐ Yes ☐ No | |
| | • Use of loose parts as symbols for familiar objects. | ☐ Yes ☐ No | |
| | • Repetition and building upon specific uses of loose parts. | ☐ Yes ☐ No | |
| **Stage 4: Elaborate Use** | • Loose parts used in problem-solving or inventive activities. | ☐ Yes ☐ No | |
| | • Integration of loose parts into larger plans and ideas. | ☐ Yes ☐ No | |
| | • Expansion and growth of children's theories and concepts. | ☐ Yes ☐ No | |

# CHAPTER 5: PLAY INVITATION PLANNER

| DATE: | | |
|---|---|---|
| **OBSERVATIONS**<br>What big ideas did you observe?<br>What did the children do? (Play schemas)<br>What did the children say? (Play narratives)<br><br>**EDUCATOR QUESTIONS**<br>What are you wondering?<br>What has your curiosity?<br><br>**INVITATION**<br>What material(s) could you add to investigate your wondering?<br><br>**REFLECTION**<br>What did you discover about the children's play schemas and big ideas?<br>What is your next step? | | |

# CHAPTER 6: LISTENING AWARENESS REFLECTION FORM

### *Level 1: Cosmetic Listening*

"I look like I'm listening, but I'm not fully with you. I'm thinking about other things right now."

Reflect on a recent interaction where you engaged in cosmetic listening. *What was the situation, and how did it feel?*

### *Level 2: Conversational Listening*

"I'm listening in order to respond. I'm thinking about what I want to say."

Reflect on a recent interaction where you engaged in conversational listening. *What was the impact on the conversation?*

### *Level 3: Active Listening*

"I'm focused on what you're saying, and you have my full attention."

Reflect on a recent interaction where you engaged in active listening. *How did it change the dynamic of the conversation?*

### *Level 4: Deep Listening*

"I'm more focused on you than me; I'm getting a sense of who you are right now."

Reflect on a recent interaction where you engaged in deep listening. *How did it make the other person feel?*

# CHAPTER 7: PRACTICES OF CONNECTION

## *Morning Practice: Sparkling Eyes*

The Sparkling Eyes education practice involves standing at the door of your classroom and greeting each child with sparkling eyes so that you make every child feel special and build a stronger connection with each student.

- To begin, prepare yourself by taking a moment to center your thoughts and focus on your intention to make each child feel valued.
- As each child approaches, make direct eye contact that says, "I am so excited you are here!" Smile and allow your eyes to light up with your joy and warmth. Imagine that your eyes are beaming with happiness to see each child.

This practice builds deeper connections, self-esteem, and a sense of inclusion, creating a classroom environment where every child feels valued. Remember, children notice if you are excited to see one child more than the others. This practice is a powerful way to make sure you are communicating with your eyes—every child matters.

## *Evening Practice: Remembering Each Child*

This practice is adapted from my Waldorf teacher training. Before going to sleep each night, take a moment to remember each child in your class. Start by picturing their faces. At first, you might forget one or two, which is okay. To help, you can count as you remember. For example, if you have eighteen children and you've only recalled fifteen, you know there are three children you haven't connected with yet.

Once you can easily recall each child's face, pick a new detail to recall about each child. Here are some that I have used:

- their hairstyle
- the color of their shoes
- the clothing they wear
- the color of their eyes
- the shape of their ears

Practice regularly to strengthen your connection with each child.

## CHAPTER 8: HARNESSING THE INNATE INTELLIGENCES OF THE WHOLE CHILD

### *The Intelligence of the Physical Self (Self-Regulation)*

- How can I integrate more physical activities into my teaching to help children develop self-regulation?
- How can I create a yes environment that balances children's need for free physical exploration with necessary safety and classroom management considerations?

### *The Intelligence of the Social/Emotional Self (Self-Awareness)*

- How can I create environments that offer a rich variety of choices while ensuring the safety and well-being of the children in my care?
- How can I support children in exploring their interests and preferences without imposing my own biases or expectations?

### *The Intelligence of the Cognitive Self (Self-Perseverance)*

- Am I supporting children in perseverance when they face frustration and challenge?

### *The Intelligence of the Embodied Self (Self-Expression)*

- What are some ways I can bring new and different art forms (like painting, storytelling, and acting) to help the children in my care play with self-expression?

# DAILY REFLECTION TOOL

Use this form to reflect on your day. If you have a coteacher, reflect together. Once you have used it a few times, the process will take under five minutes.

## The Six-Point Daily Reflection

| DATE: | |
|---|---|
| 1. What worked really well today? | |
| 2. What did not work or could have been more effective? What was missing or needed? | |
| 3. Which children stood out today? Who captured my attention? Why? | |
| 4. What is important for me to do tomorrow? This week? | |
| 5. If I had to pick a word or phrase for today, what would it be? | |
| 6. Anything else? | |

# References


Athey, Chris. 2007. *Extending Thought in Young Children: A Parent-Teacher Partnership*. 2nd ed. SAGE Publications.

Ayres, A. Jean. 2005. *Sensory Integration and the Child*. 25th ed. Western Psychological Services.

Bolin, Stephanie. 2015. "A Study of Stimulating Versus Non-Stimulating Visuals in a Preschool Classroom." *Journal of Interdisciplinary Undergraduate Research* 7 (article 4). https://knowledge.e.southern.edu/jiur/vol7/iss1/4.

Bonafede, Carmen, and Elna van der Merwe. 2023. "Normal Ranges for Proprioceptive Tasks in 6-Year-Old Children in Mangaung. *South African Journal of Childhood*. 13 (1): a1243. https://doi.org/10.4102/sajce.v13i1.1243.

Brown, Brené. 2013. "Shame vs. Guilt." Brené Brown, January 15. https://brenebrown.com/articles/2013/01/15/shame-v-guilt.

Brown, Stuart L., and Christopher C. Vaughan. 2009. *Play: How It Shapes the Brain, Opens the Imagination, and Invigorates the Soul*. Avery.

Brownlee, Pennie. 2016. *The Sacred Urge to Play: Unfolding Your Child's Intelligence, Imagination, Creativity, and Joy for Life*. Good Egg Books.

Burns, Martha S. 2012. "The New Brain Science of Learning." TED Talk, Enola, PA, February 1. 27 min., 41 sec. www.youtube.com/watch?v=ahSYwchh-QM.

Cameron, Julia. 2016. *The Artist's Way: A Spiritual Path for Higher Creativity*. 30th ed. TarcherPerigee.

Carr, Margaret, and Wendy Lee. 2019. *Learning Stories in Practice*. SAGE Publications.

Center on the Developing Child at Harvard University. 2025. "Serve and Return." Accessed January 17. https://developingchild.harvard.edu/science/key-concepts/serve-and-return/.

Chatterjee, Rhitu. 2024. "Again! Again! Here's Why Toddlers Love to Do Things on Repeat." NPR.org. January 12. www.npr.org/sections/health-shots/2024/01/12/1224352481toddlers-repetitive-play-repeat-brain-development.

Chilton-Pearce, Joseph. 1998. Rahima Baldwin's Homeschooling Conference. Boulder, Colorado.

Christakis, Dimitri A., Frederick J. Zimmerman, David L. DiGiuseppe, and Carolyn A. McCarty. 2004. "Early Television Exposure and Subsequent Attentional Problems in Children." *Pediatrics* 113 (4): 708–13.

Cleverley, John, and D. C. Phillips. 1987. *Visions of Childhood: Influential Models from Locke to Spock*. Allen & Unwin.

Coelho, Paul. 2019. "The Dirty Laundry," *Paulo Coelho* (blog), September 9. https://paulocoelhoblog.com/2019/09/25/the-dirty-laundry.

Colliver, Y., J. Harrison, J. E. Brown, and P. Humburg. 2022. "Free Play Predicts Self-Regulation Years Later: Longitudinal Evidence from a Large Australian Sample of Toddlers and Preschoolers." *Early Childhood Research Quarterly* 59, 2nd quarter: 148–61.

Curtis, Deb, and Nadia Jaboneta. 2019. *Children's Lively Minds: Schema Theory made Visible*. Redleaf Press.

Davis, K., Christodoulou, J., Seider, S., and Gardner, H. 2011. "The Theory of Multiple Intelligences." In *Cambridge Handbook of Intelligence*, edited by R. J. Sternberg and S. B. Kaufman. Cambridge University Press.

Diamond, Adele. 2013. "Executive Functions." *Annual Review of Psychology* 64: 135–68.

Drummond, Tom. 2020. "Conversations with Children." Interview by Sally Haughey. The Pedagogy of Play Conference, Fairy Dust Teaching Online Platform, January.

Ezell, Margaret J. M. 1983. "John Locke's Images of Childhood: Early Eighteenth Century Response to Some Thoughts Concerning Education. *Eighteenth-Century Studies* 17 (2): 139–55.

Godin, Seth. 2012. "Stop Stealing Dreams (What Is School For?)." *Seth's Blog*. https://seths.blog/wp-content/uploads/2019/05/stop-stealing-dreams6print.pdf.

Goldberg H. 2022. "Growing Brains, Nurturing Minds-Neuroscience as an Educational Tool to Support Students' Development as Life-Long Learners." *Brain Science* 12 (November 26): 1622.

Hannaford, Carla. 1995. *Smart Moves: Why Learning Is Not All in Your Head*. Great Ocean Publishers.

Hart, Betty, and Todd R. Risley. 2003. "The Early Catastrophe: The 30 Million Word Gap by Age 3." *American Educator* 27 (1): 4–9.

Hattie, John. 2009. *Visible Learning: A Synthesis of Over 800 Meta-Analyses Relating to Achievement*. Routledge.

Heitzenrater, Richard P. 2001. "John Wesley and Children." In *The Child in Christian Thought*, edited by Marcia J. Bunge. Eerdmans.

Hintzman, Douglas L. 1976. "Repetition and Memory." In *Psychology of Learning and Motivation*, edited by Gordon H. Bower. Vol. 10. Academic Press.

Jackson, Philip W. 1990. *Life in Classrooms*. Teachers College Press.

Kashin, Diane. 2023. "What's the Big Idea? Children's Interests That Make a Difference." *Technology Rich Inquiry Based Research* (blog). February 23. https://tecribresearch.blog/2023/02/26.

Kohli, Preeti, Zachary M. Soler, Shaun A. Nguyen, John S. Muus, and Rodney J. Schlosser. 2016. "The Association Between Olfaction and Depression: A Systematic Review." *Chemical Senses* 41 (6): 479–86. https://doi.org/10.1093/chemse/bjw061.

Kohn, Alfie. 1999. *Punished by Rewards: The Trouble with Gold Stars, Incentive Plans, A's, Praise, and Other Bribes*. Houghton Mifflin Harcourt.

Kovalik, Susan. 2001. *Exceeding Expectations: A User's Guide to Implementing Brain Research in the Classroom*. 2nd ed. Books for Educators.

Kranowitz, Carol. 2022. *The Out-of-Sync Child: Recognizing and Coping with Sensory Processing Differences*. 3rd ed. TarcherPerigee.

Kranowitz, Carol, and Joye Newman. 2010. *Growing an In-Sync Child: Simple, Fun Activities to Help Every Child Develop, Learn, and Grow*. Penguin Group.

Kryczka, Cathie. 2021. "Again, Again! Why Your Kid Wants to Do the Same Activity Over and Over." *Today's Parent*, March 10. www.todaysparent.com/toddler/kids-repetition.

Lervåg, Arne, Charles Hulme, and Monica Melby-Lervåg. 2017. "Unpicking the Developmental Relationship Between Oral Language Skills and Reading Comprehension: It's Simple, but Complex." *Child Development* 89 (5): 1821–38. https://doi.org/10.1111/cdev.12861.

Lillard, Angeline S., and Jennifer Peterson. 2011. "The Immediate Impact of Different Types of Television on Young Children's Executive Function." *Pediatrics* 128 (4): 644–49.

López-Gil, José Francisco, Arthur Eumann Mesas, Celia Álvarez-Bueno, Carlos Pascual-Morena, Alicia Saz-Lara, and Ivan Cavero-Redondo. 2022. "Association Between Eating Habits and Perceived School Performance: A Cross-Sectional Study Among 46,455 Adolescents From 42 Countries." *Frontiers in Nutrition* 9 (February 3): 797415. https://doi.org/10.3389/fnut.2022.797415.

Malaguzzi, Loris. 1994. "Your Image of the Child: Where Teaching Begins." *Exchange* 96: 52–56.

May-Benson, Teresa, Juliana Lopes de Mello Gentil, and Alison Teasdale. 2020. "Characteristics and Prevalence of Gravitational Insecurity in Children with Sensory Processing Dysfunction." *Research in Development* 101 (June): https://doi.org/10.1016/j.ridd.2020.103640.

Moberg, Paul J., Vidyulata A. Kamath, Dana M. Marchetto, et al. 2014. "Meta-Analysis of Olfactory Function in Schizophrenia, First-Degree Family Members, and Youths At-Risk for Psychosis." *Schizophrenia Bulletin* 40 (1): 50–59. https://doi.org/10.1093/schbul/sbt049.

Panksepp, Jaak. 1998. *Affective Neuroscience: The Foundations of Human and Animal Emotions*. Oxford University Press.

Pica, Rae. 2015. "Debunking the Belief That Earlier Is Better." RaePica.com. www.raepica.com/2015/12/the-value-of-play-in-early-childhood.

Robinson, Sir Ken. 2006. "Do Schools Kill Creativity?" TED Talk, February. www.ted.com/talks/sir_ken_robinson_do_schools_kill_creativity /transcript.

Rolland, Rebecca. 2022. *The Art of Talking with Children: The Simple Keys to Nurturing Kindness, Creativity, and Confidence in Kids*. HarperOne.

Romeo, Rachel R., Julia A. Leonard, Hannah M. Grotzinger, et al. 2021. "Neuroplasticity Associated with Changes in Conversational Turn-Taking Following a Family-Based Intervention." *Developmental Cognitive Neuroscience* 49. https://doi.org/10.1016/j.dcn.2021.100967.

Samples, Bob. 1987. *Openmind Wholemind: Parenting and Teaching Tomorrow's Children Today*. Jalmar Press.

Sjöstrand, Christina, Ivanka Savic, Eva Laudon-Meyer, Lena Hillert, Karin Lodin, and Elisabet Waldenlind. 2010. "Migraine and Olfactory Stimuli." *Current Pain and Headache Reports* 14 (3): 244–51. https://doi.org/10.1007 /s11916-010-0109-7.

Snow, Catherine E., and Diane E. Beals. 2006. "Mealtime Talk That Supports Literacy Development." *New Directions for Child and Adolescent Development* 2006 (111): 51–66. https://doi.org/10.1002/cd.155.

Spence, Charles. 2021. "The Scent of Attraction and the Smell of Success: Crossmodal Influences on Person Perception." *Cognitive Research: Principles and Implications* 6 (June): 46. https://doi:10.1186/s41235-00311-3.

Starr, Julie. 2023. *Brilliant Coaching: Become a Manager Who Can Coach*. 4th ed. Pearson Business.

Steiner, Rudolf. 1958. *Man as a Being of Sense and Perception*. Anthroposophical Publishing.

———. 1995. *The Kingdom of Childhood*. Steiner Books.

———. 2004. *Teaching Language Arts in the Waldorf School*. AWSNA.

Tyng, Chai M., U. Amin Hafeez, N. M. Saad Mohamad, S. Malik Aamir. 2017. "Influences of Emotion on Learning and Memory." *Frontiers in Psychology* 8 (August 24): https://doi.org/10.3389/fpsyg.2017.01454.

United Nations General Assembly. 1989. "Convention on the Rights of the Child." *United Nations Treaty Series* 1577 (November): 3–178. www.ohchr.org/en/instruments-mechanisms/instruments/convention-rights-child.

Weisleder, Adriana, and Anne Fernald. 2013. "Talking to Children Matters: Early Language Experience Strengthens Processing and Builds Vocabulary." *Psychological Science* 24 (11): 2143–52.

Whitaker, Daniel. 2020. "The Image of the Child." Education Hub, March 17. https://theeducationhub.org.nz/the-image-of-the-child.

Witt, Kate M., David N. Harper, and Bart A. Ellenbroek. 2024. "The Role of the Dopamine D1 Receptor in Anticipatory Pleasure and Social Play." *Neuropharmacology* 264 (February 15): 110225. https://doi.org/10.1016/j.neuropharm.2024.110225.

# INDEX

## F



## G



## H



## I

## S

## T



## U



## V

## W



## Y